Abstraction for Coloring

Hey everyone,
not gonna lie to you.
This is my 1st coloring book.
So if you like it, Great!
If you don't like it, Great!
I want to hear about it!
@stoiarichard

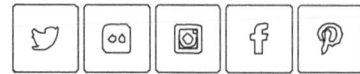

Read Me!

Feel free to color me!

Remember, always use scrap paper under your work if you are going to use markers.

All rights reserved. No part of this book may be reproduced or transmitted by any form or by any means, electronic or mechanical, including photocopy, recording, or any information storage or retrieval system, without prior written consent from the author.

©2016 Richard Stoia
www.stoiarichard.com

I0468650

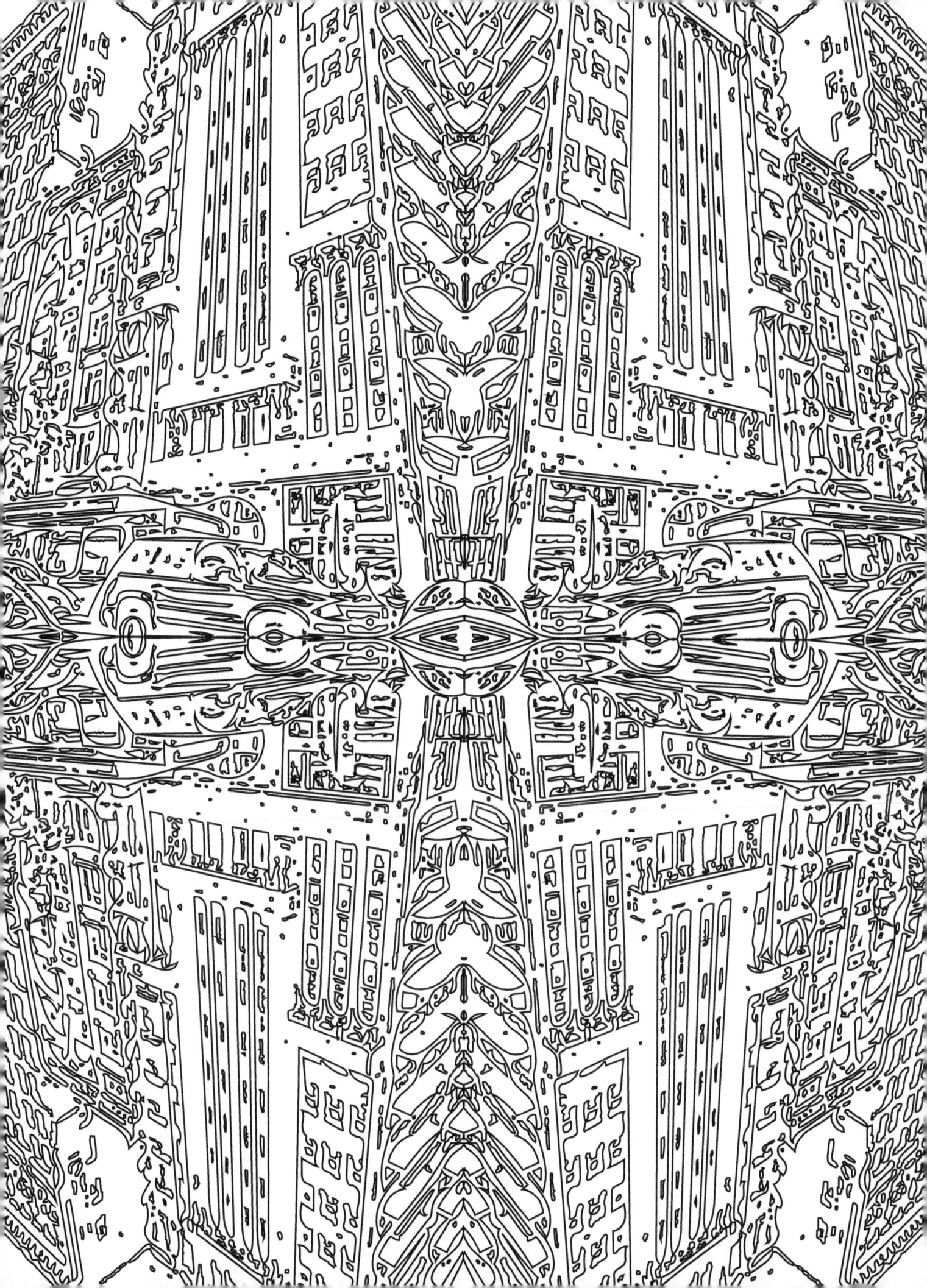

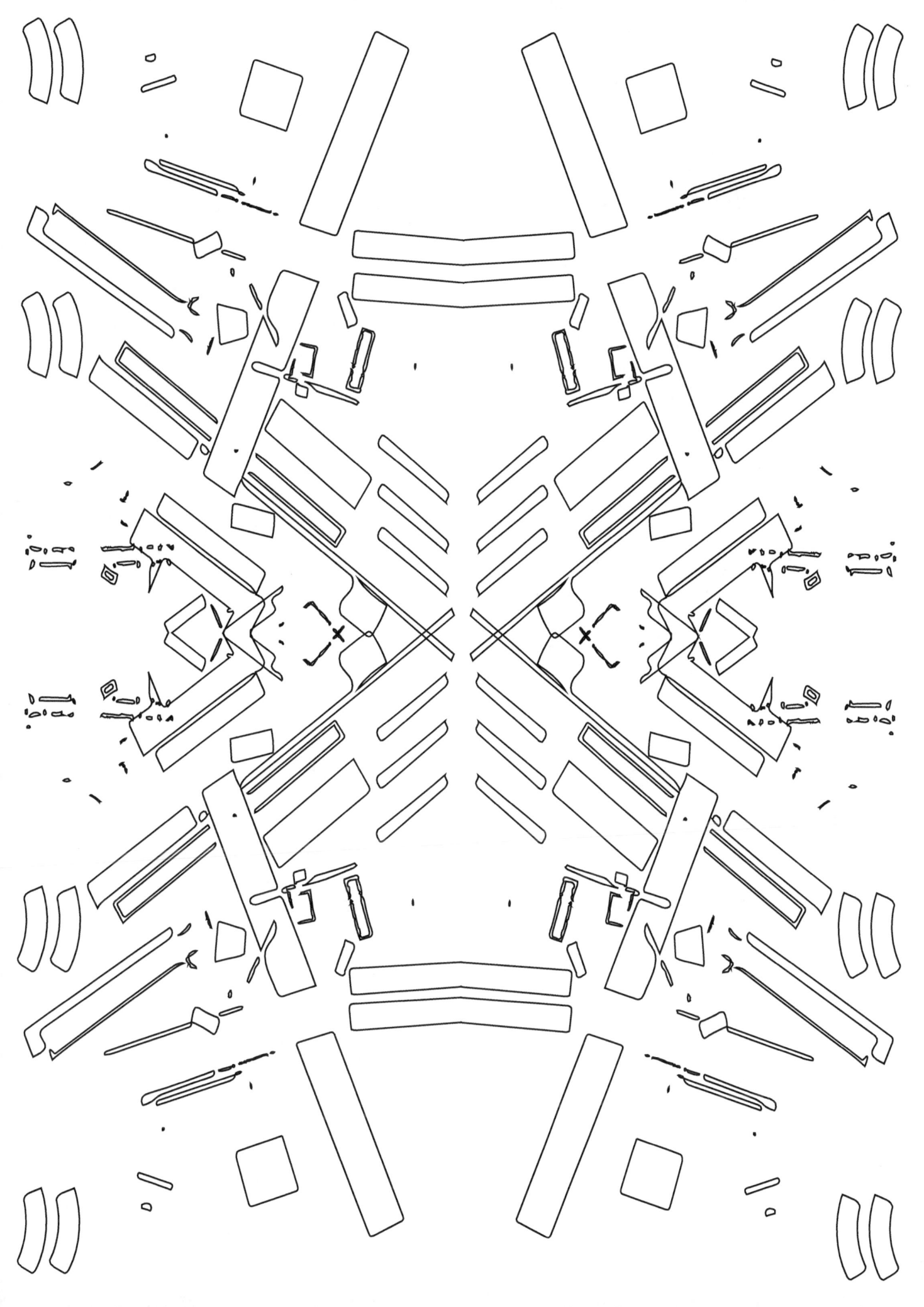

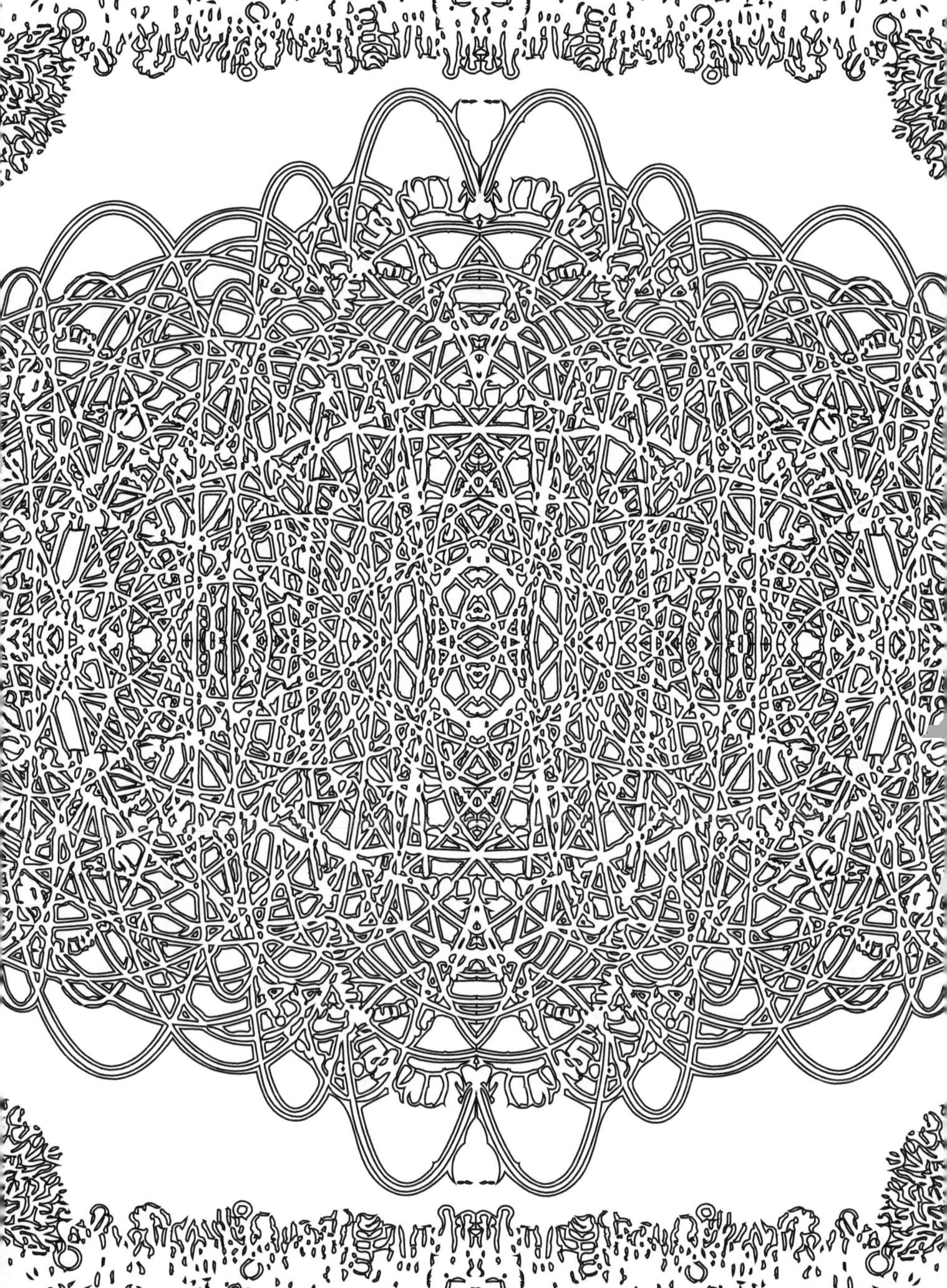

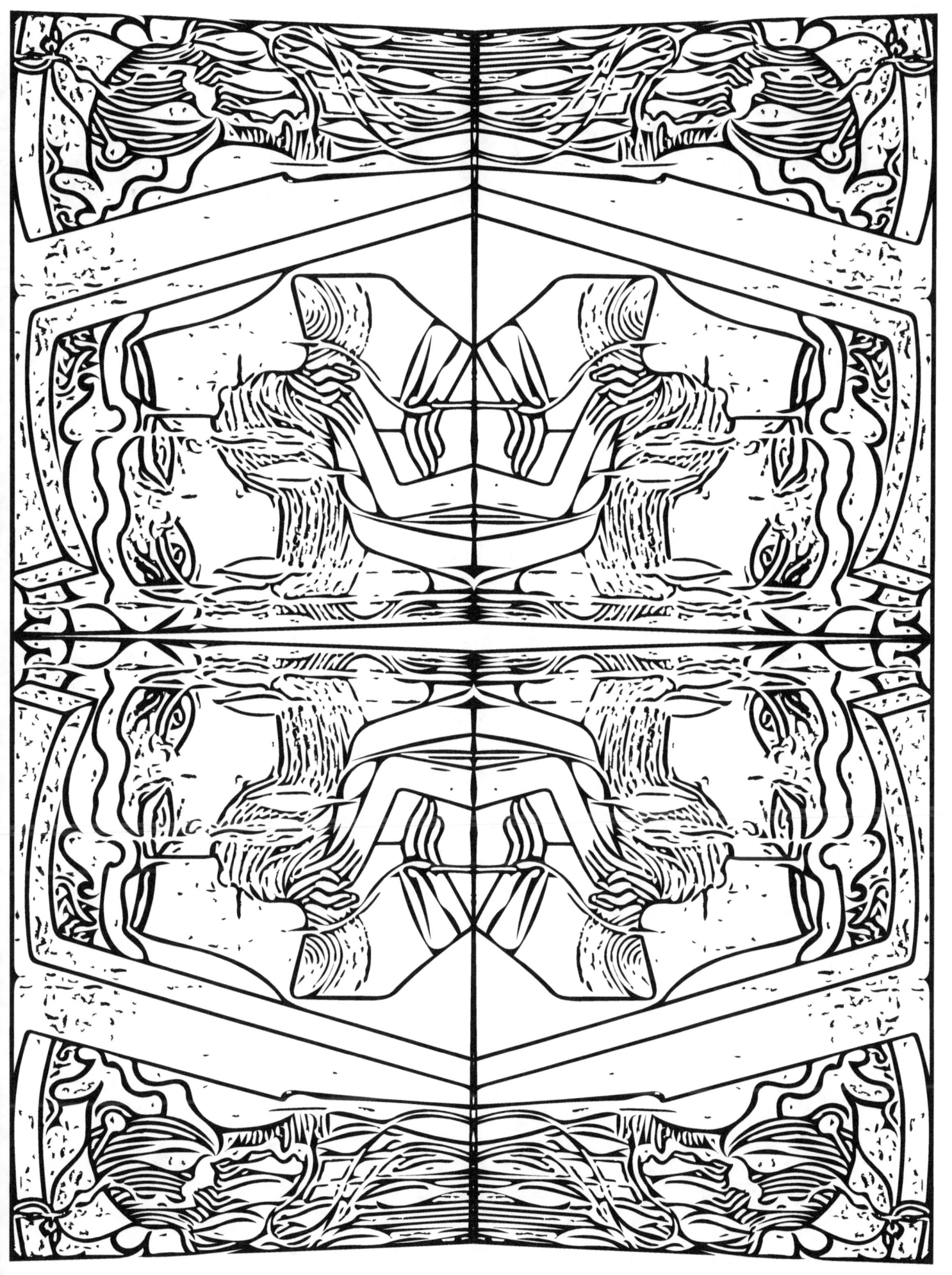

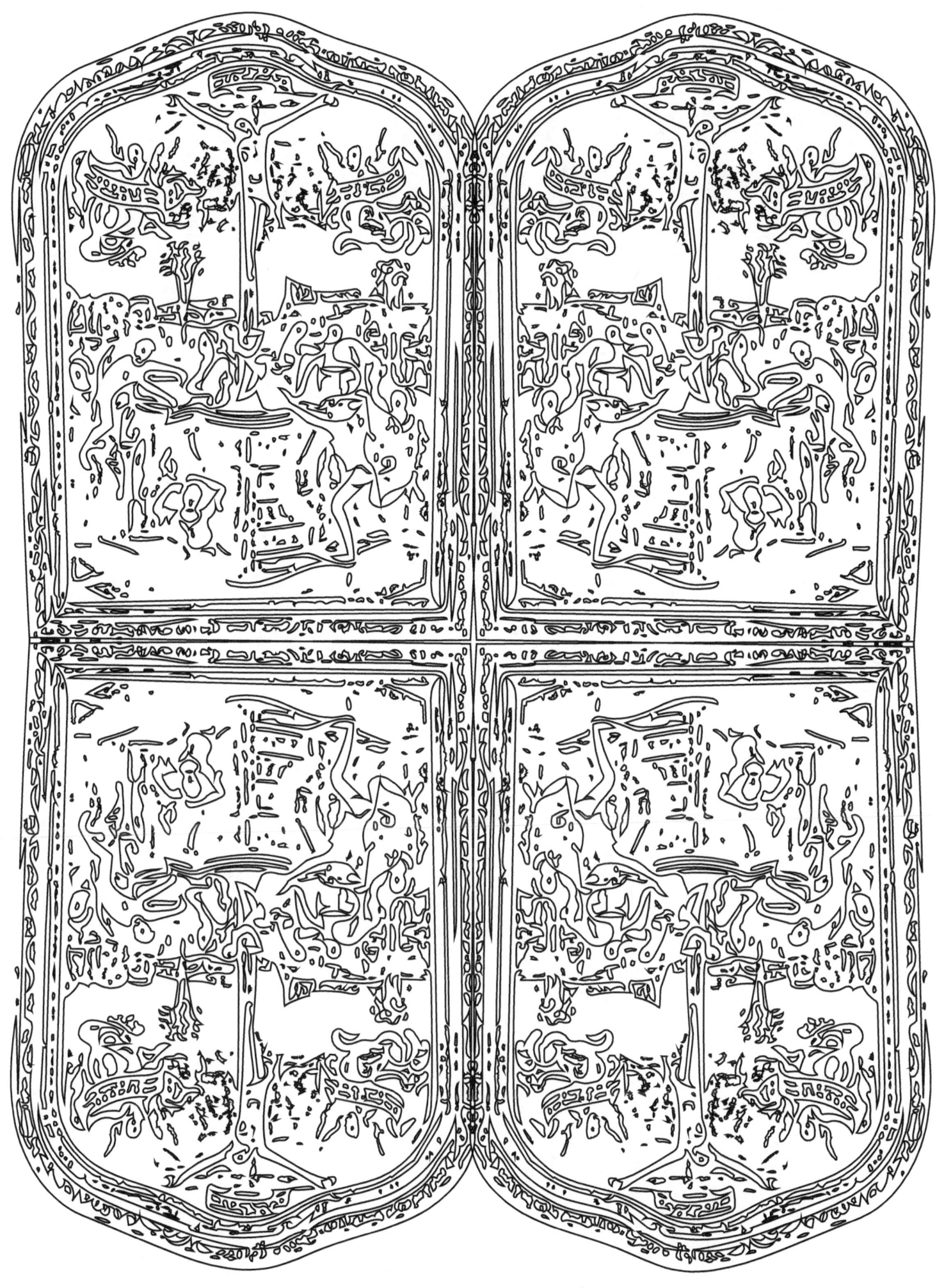

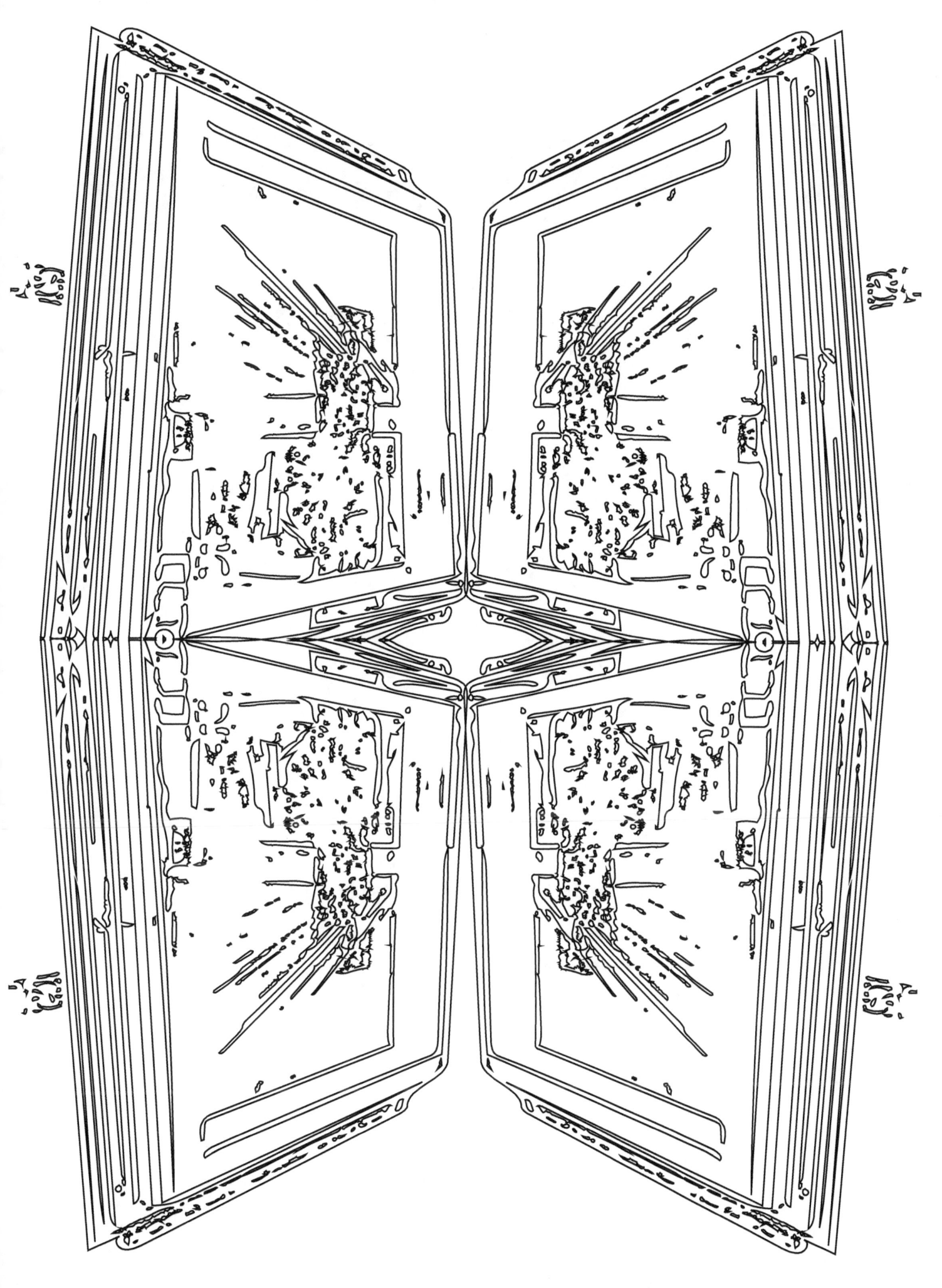

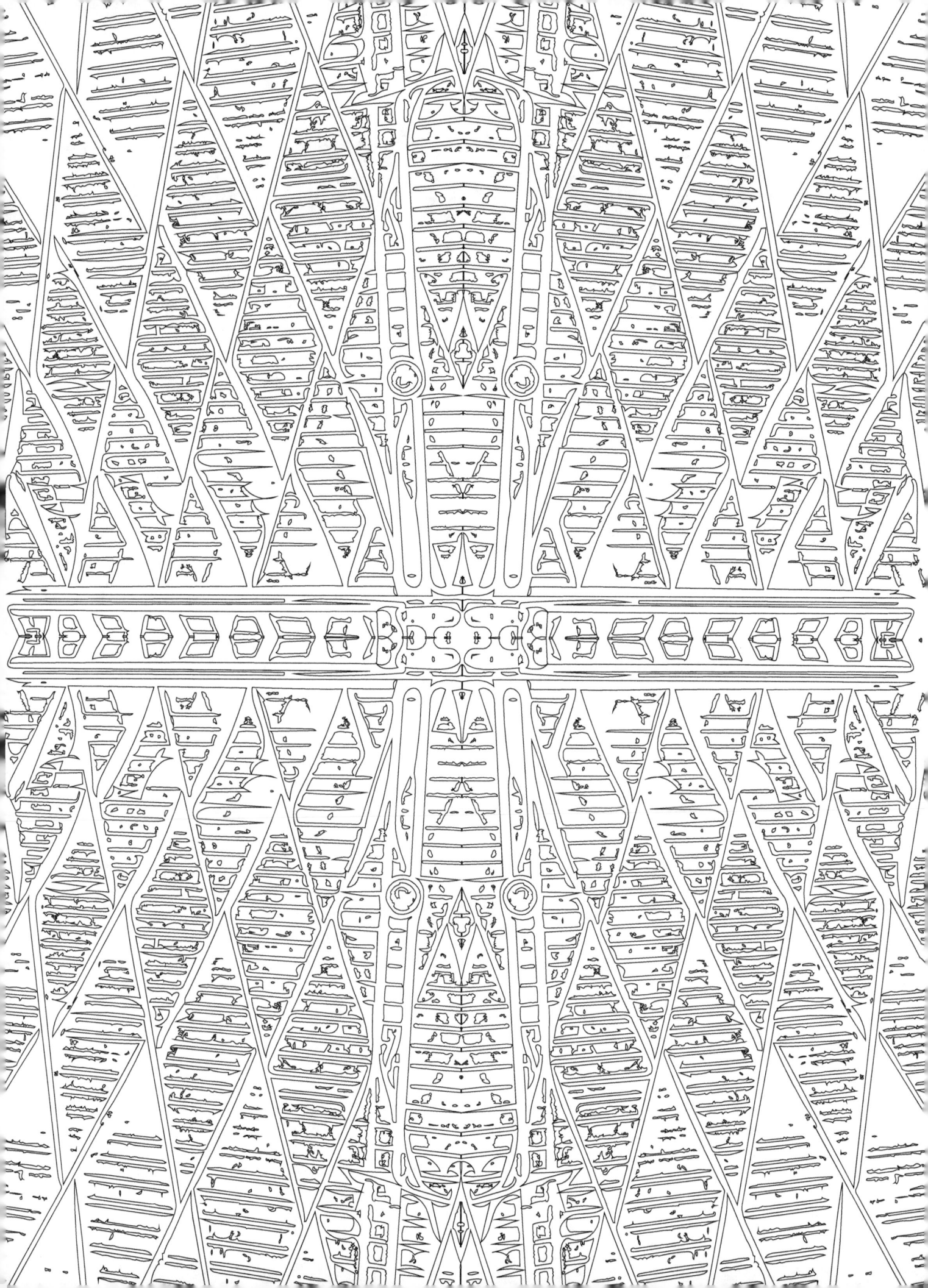

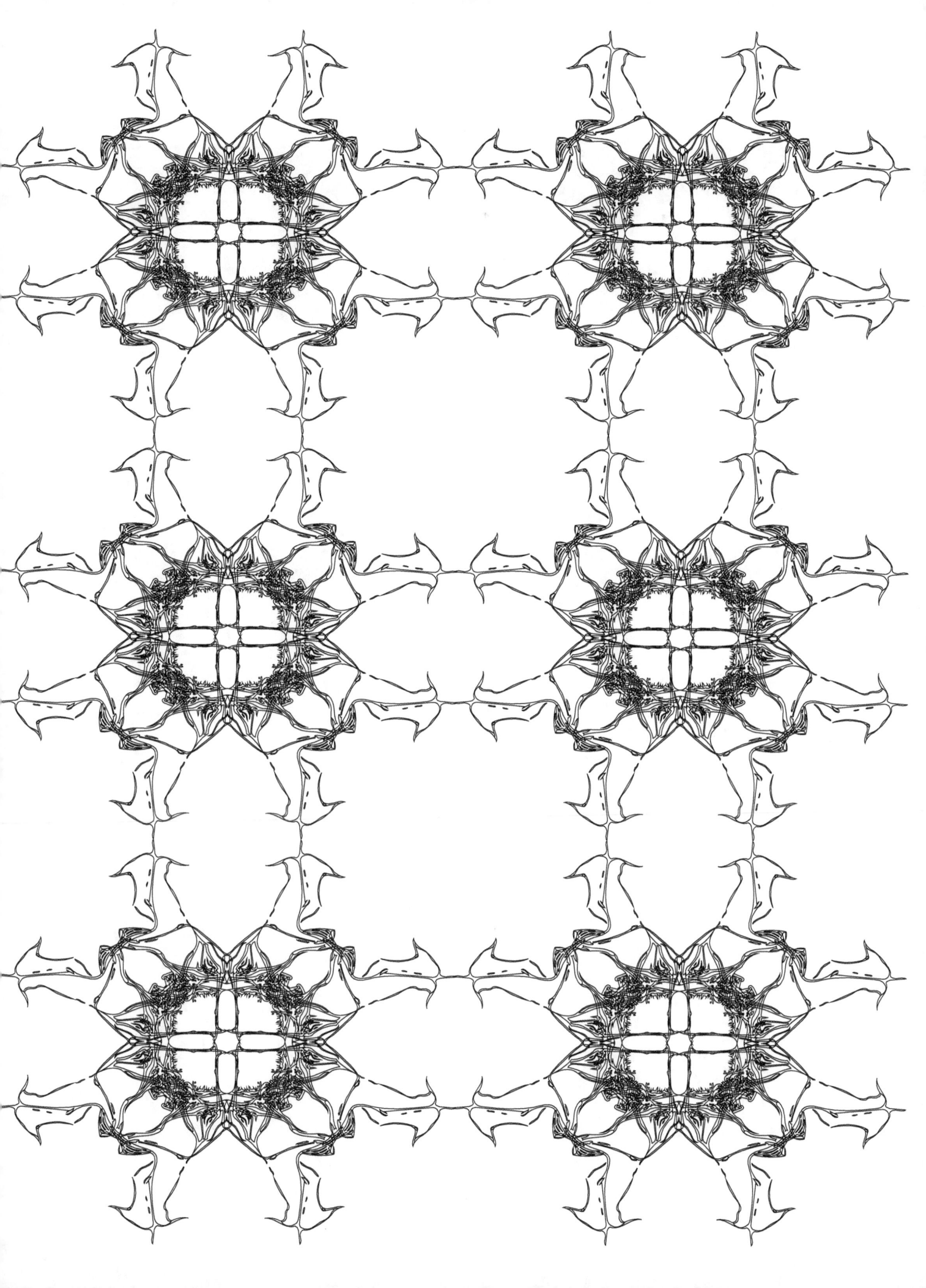

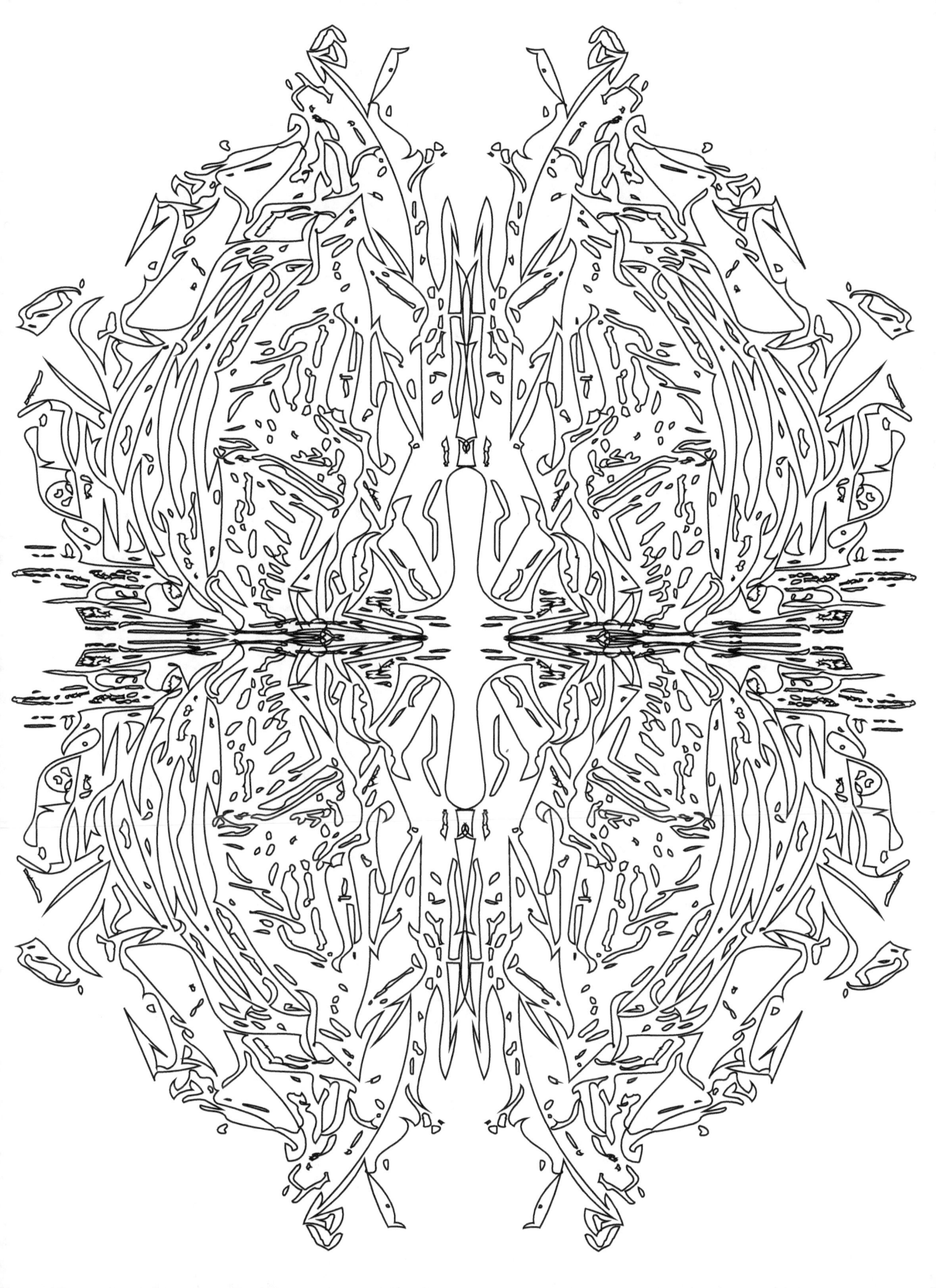

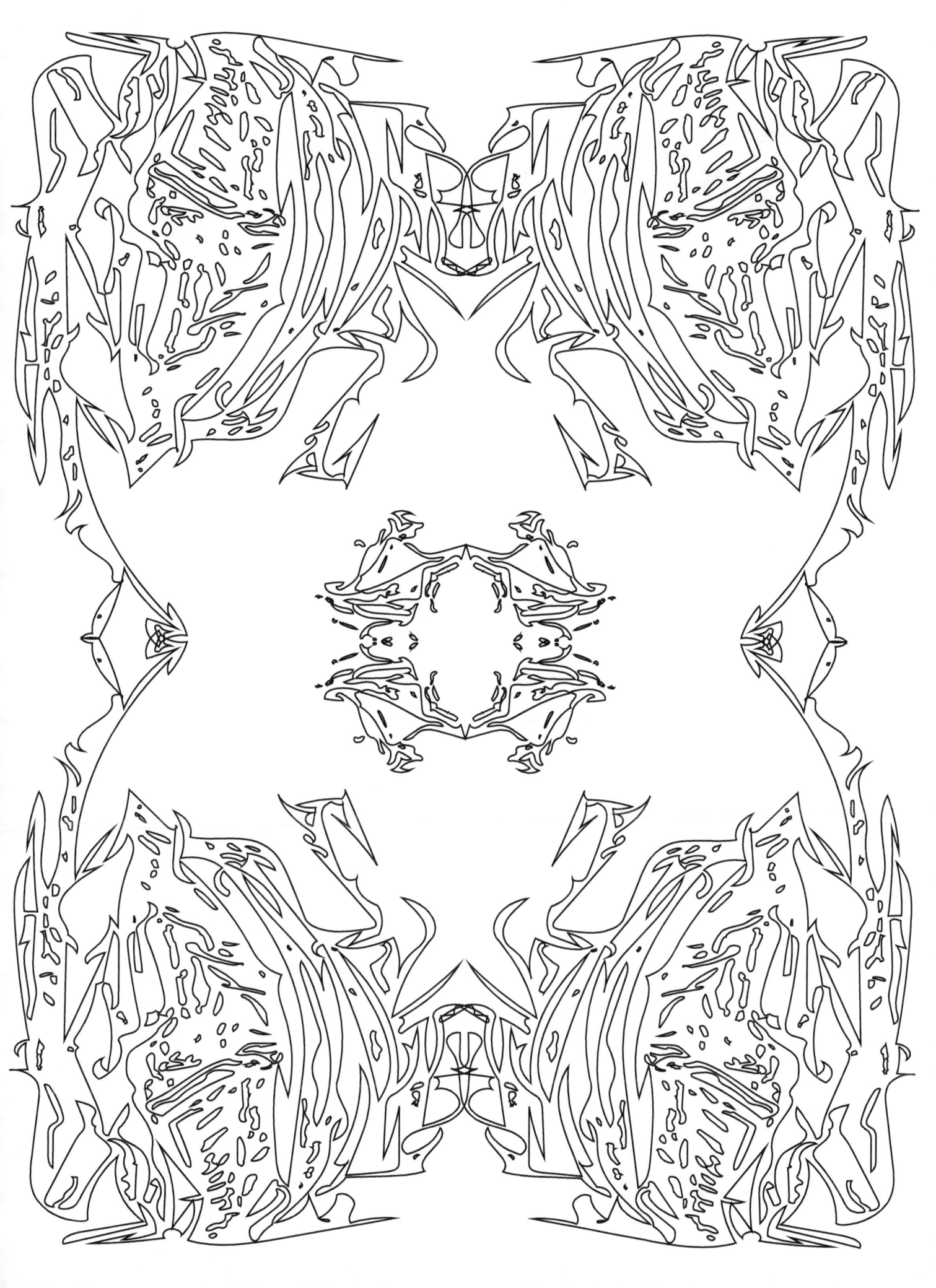

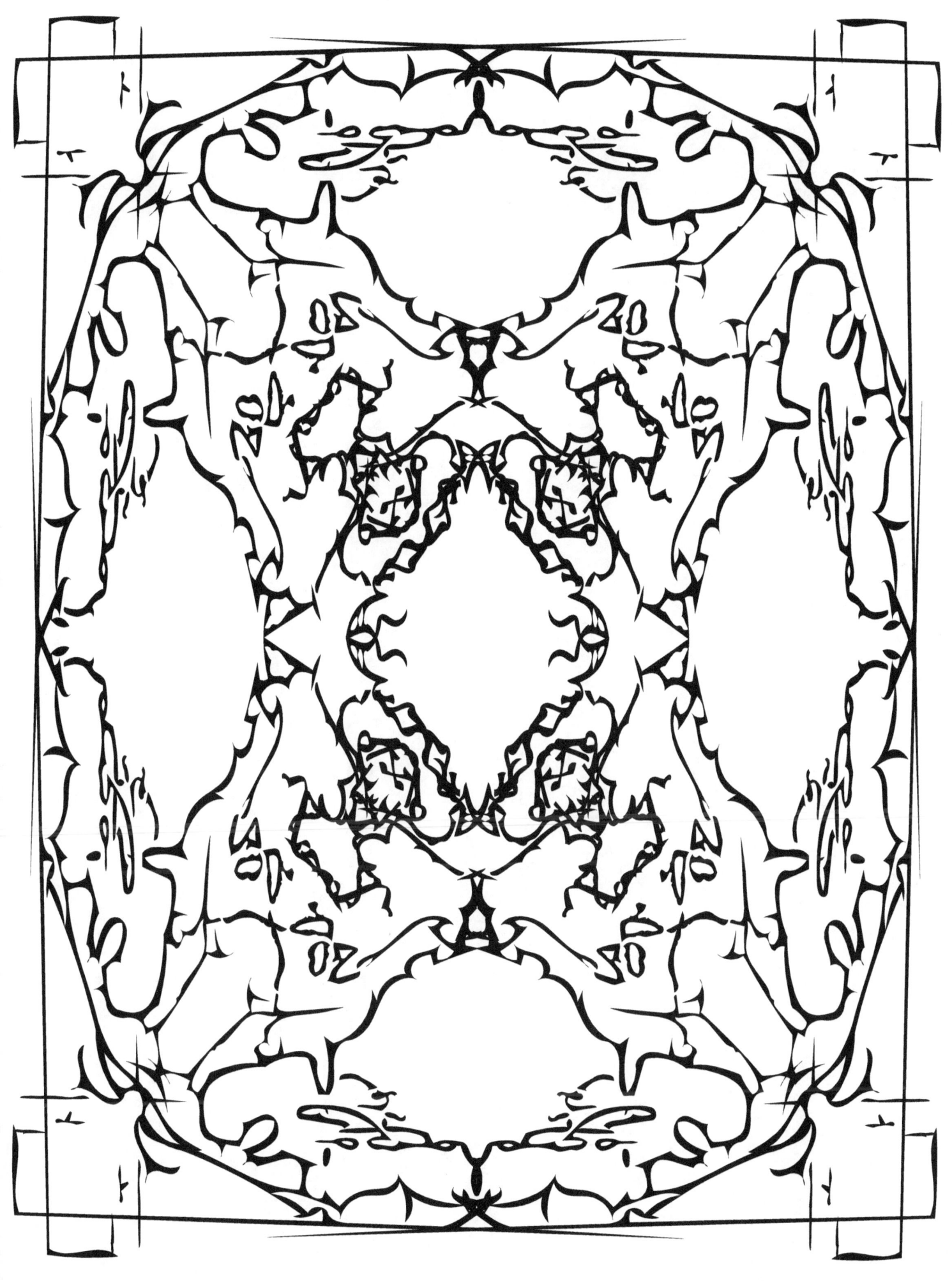

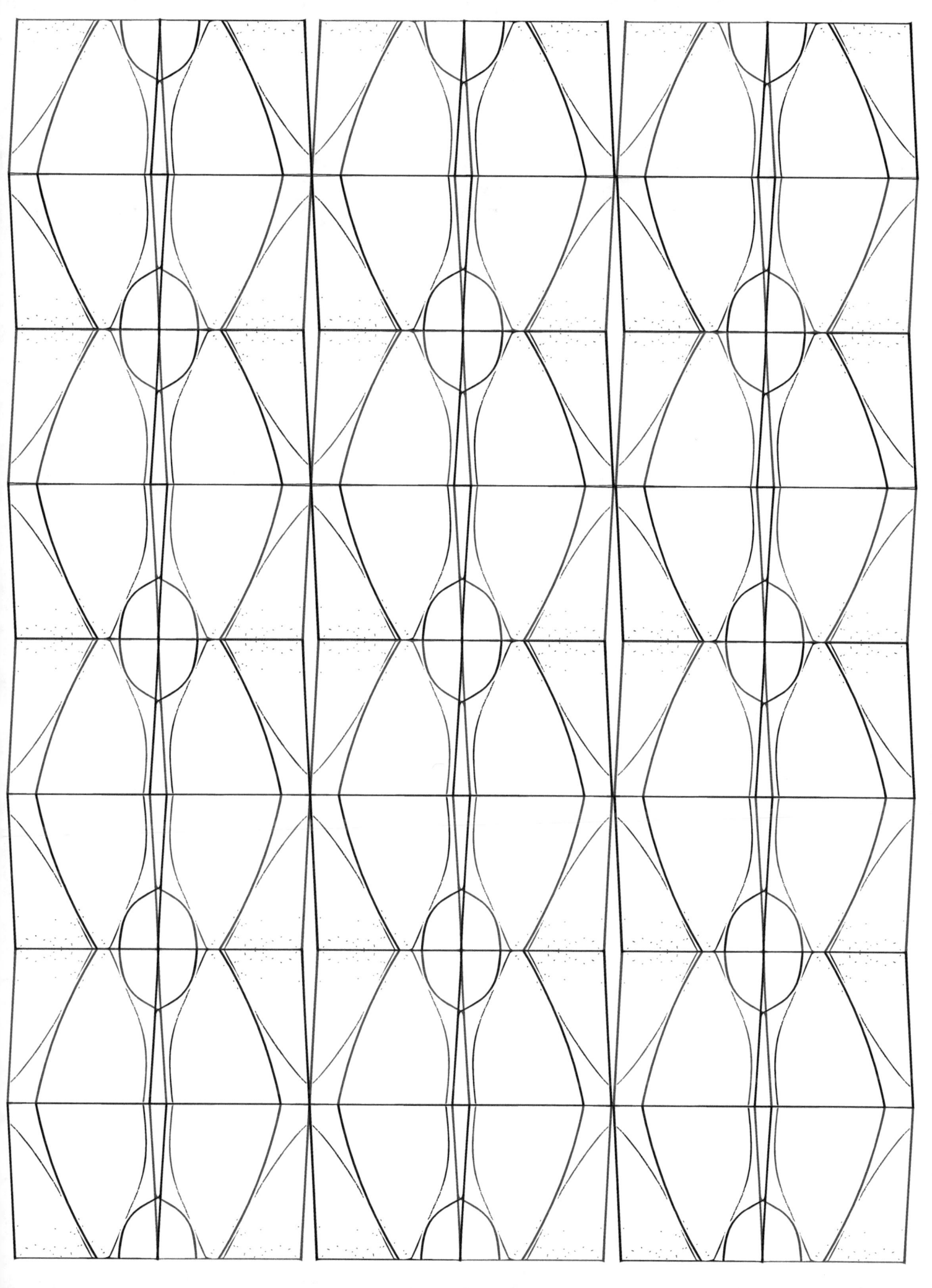

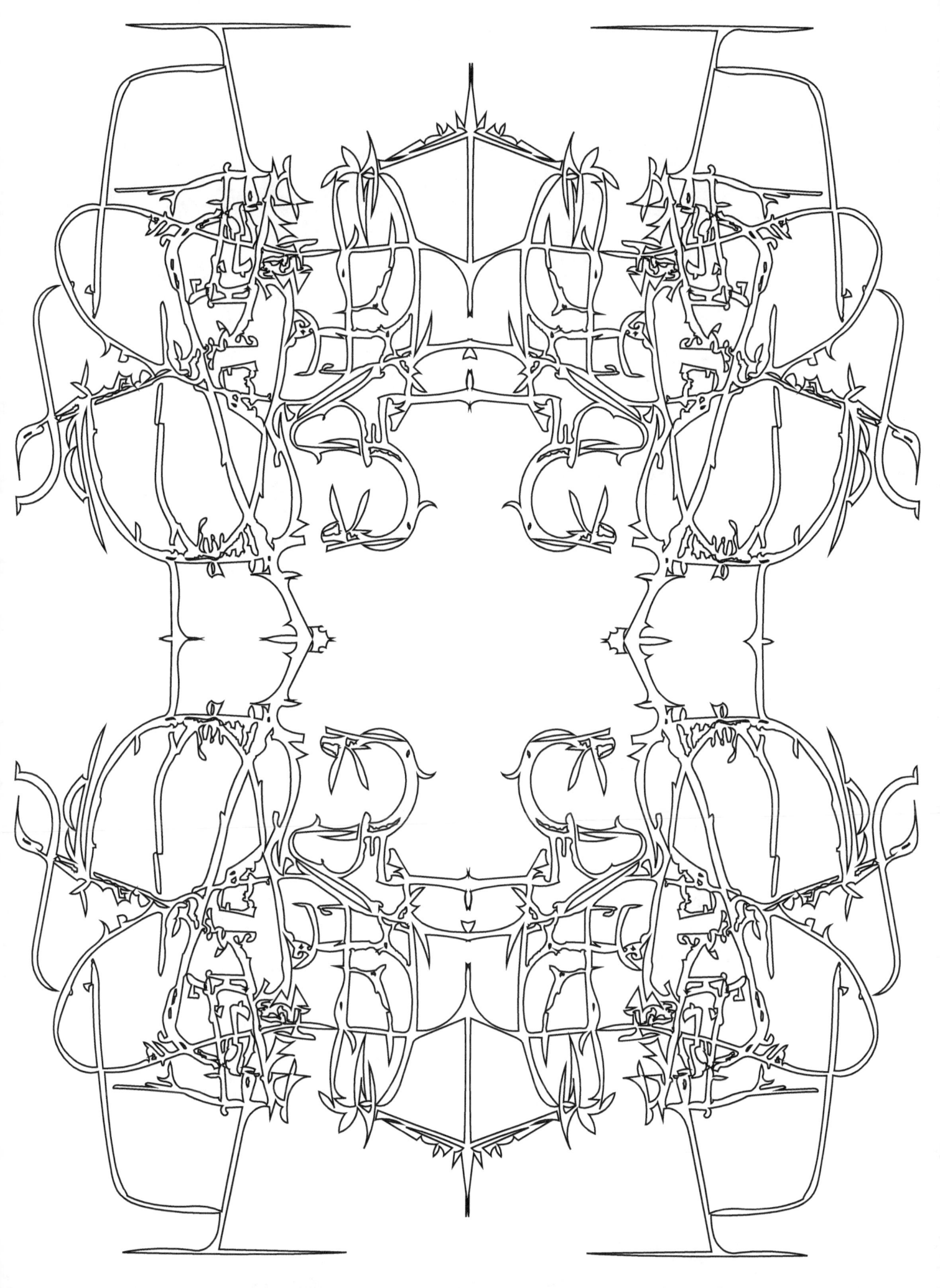

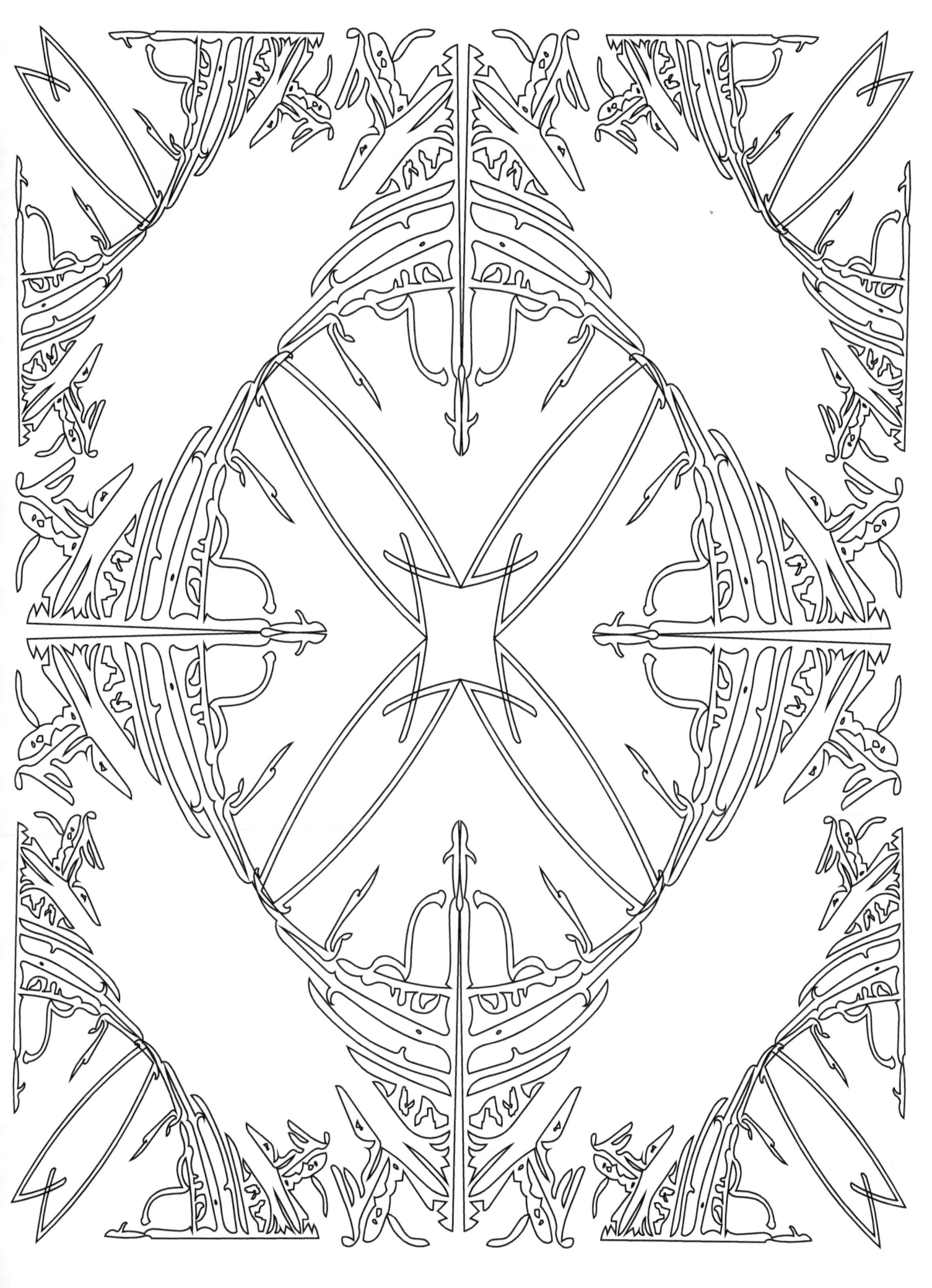

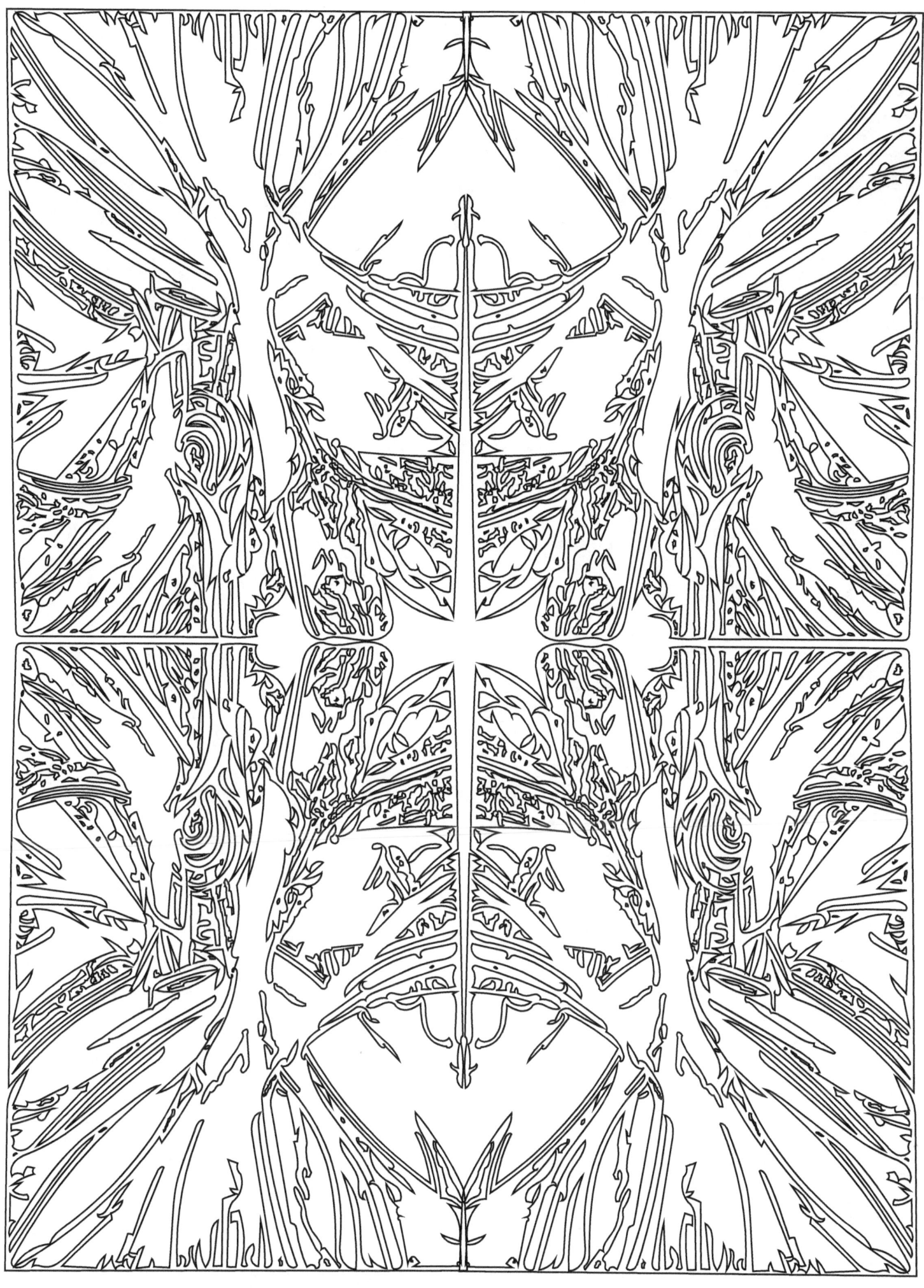

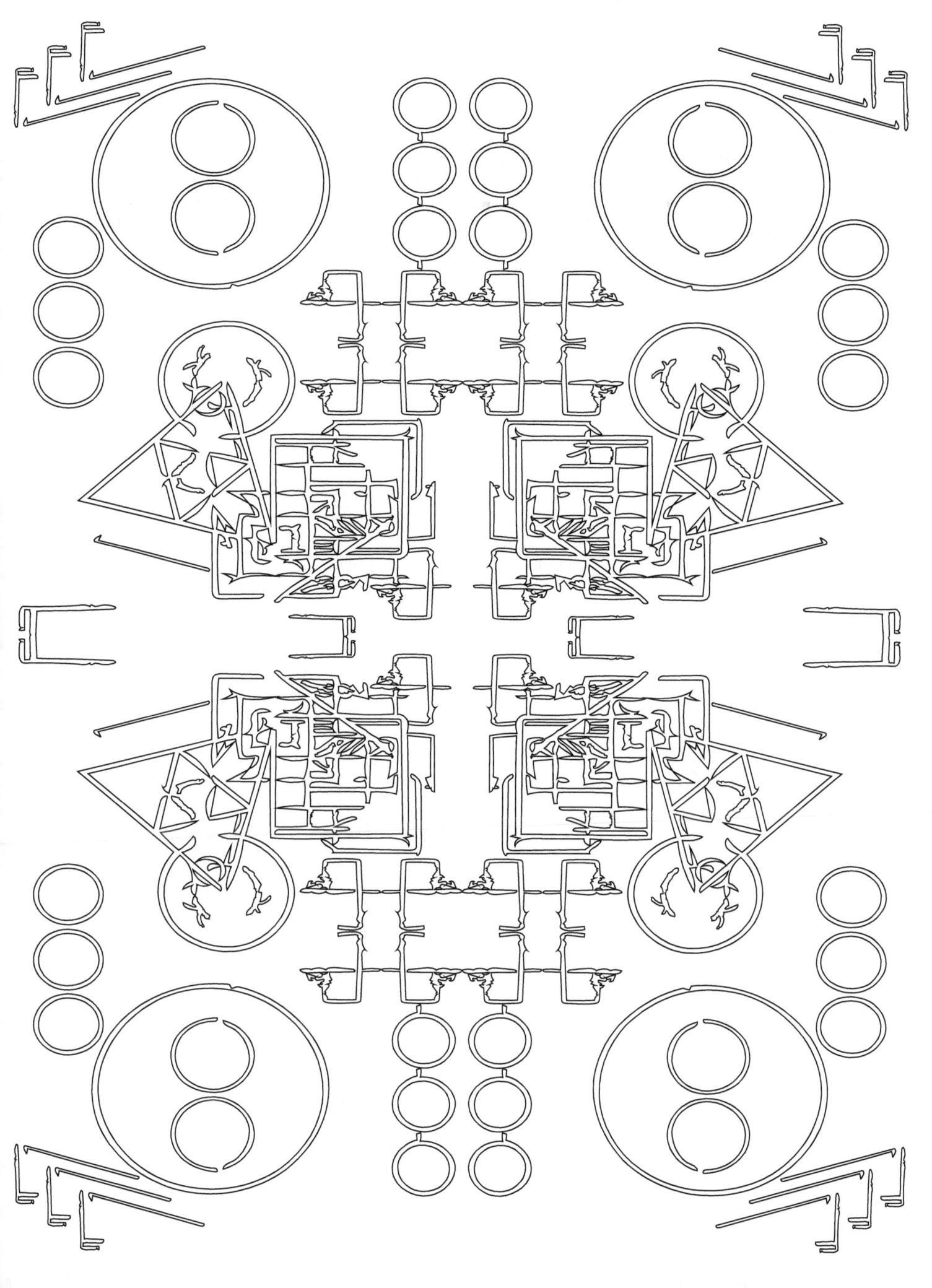

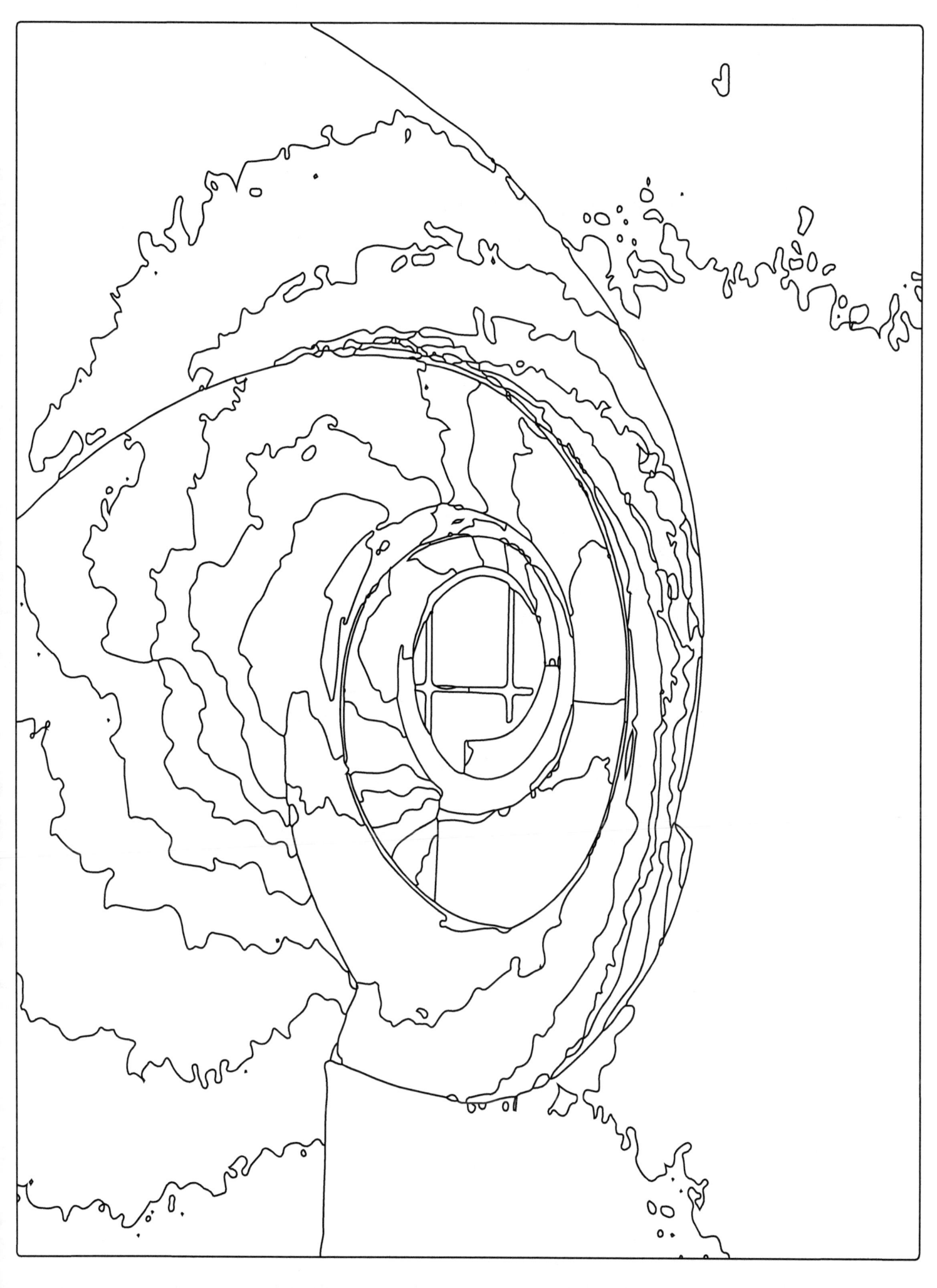

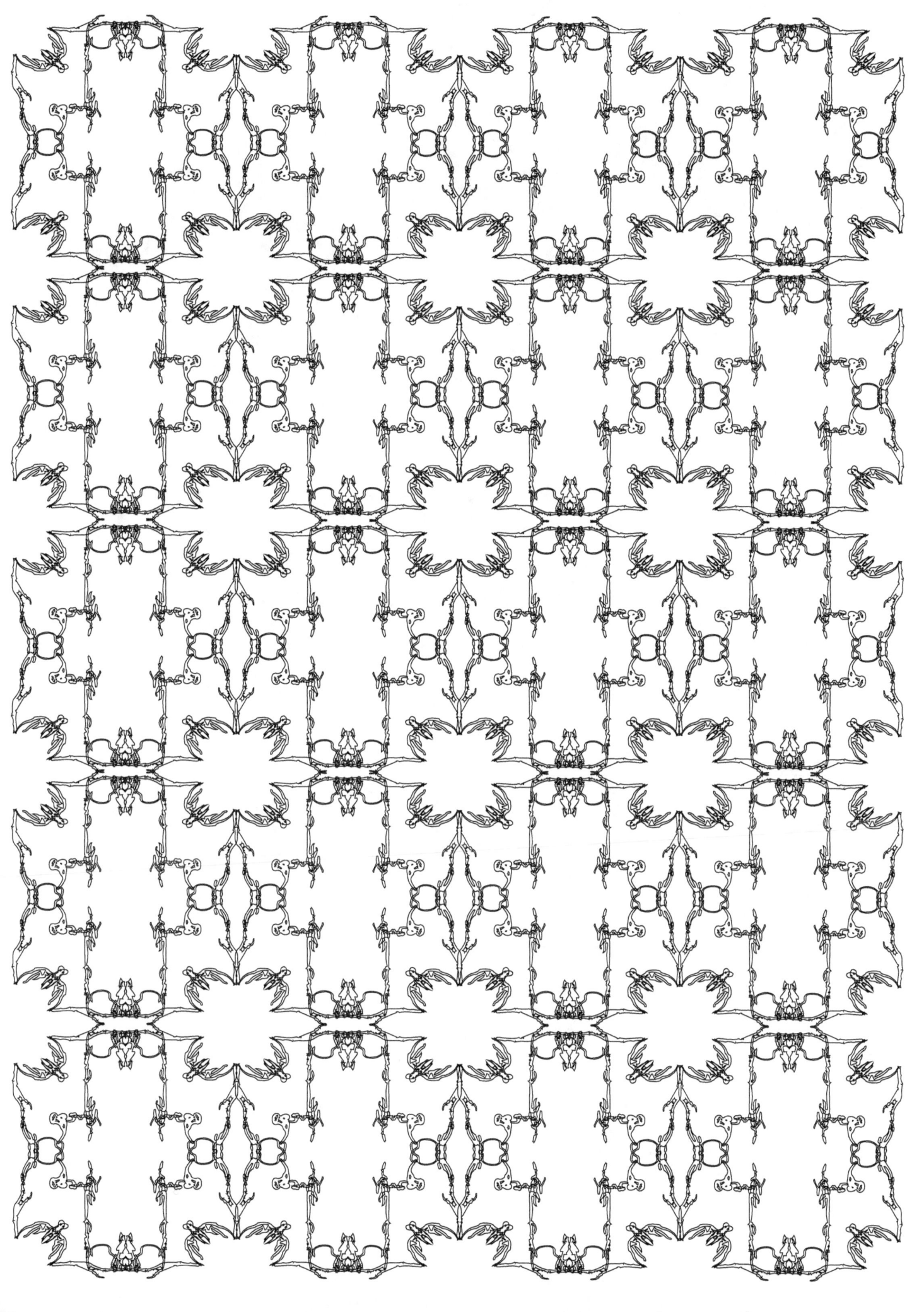

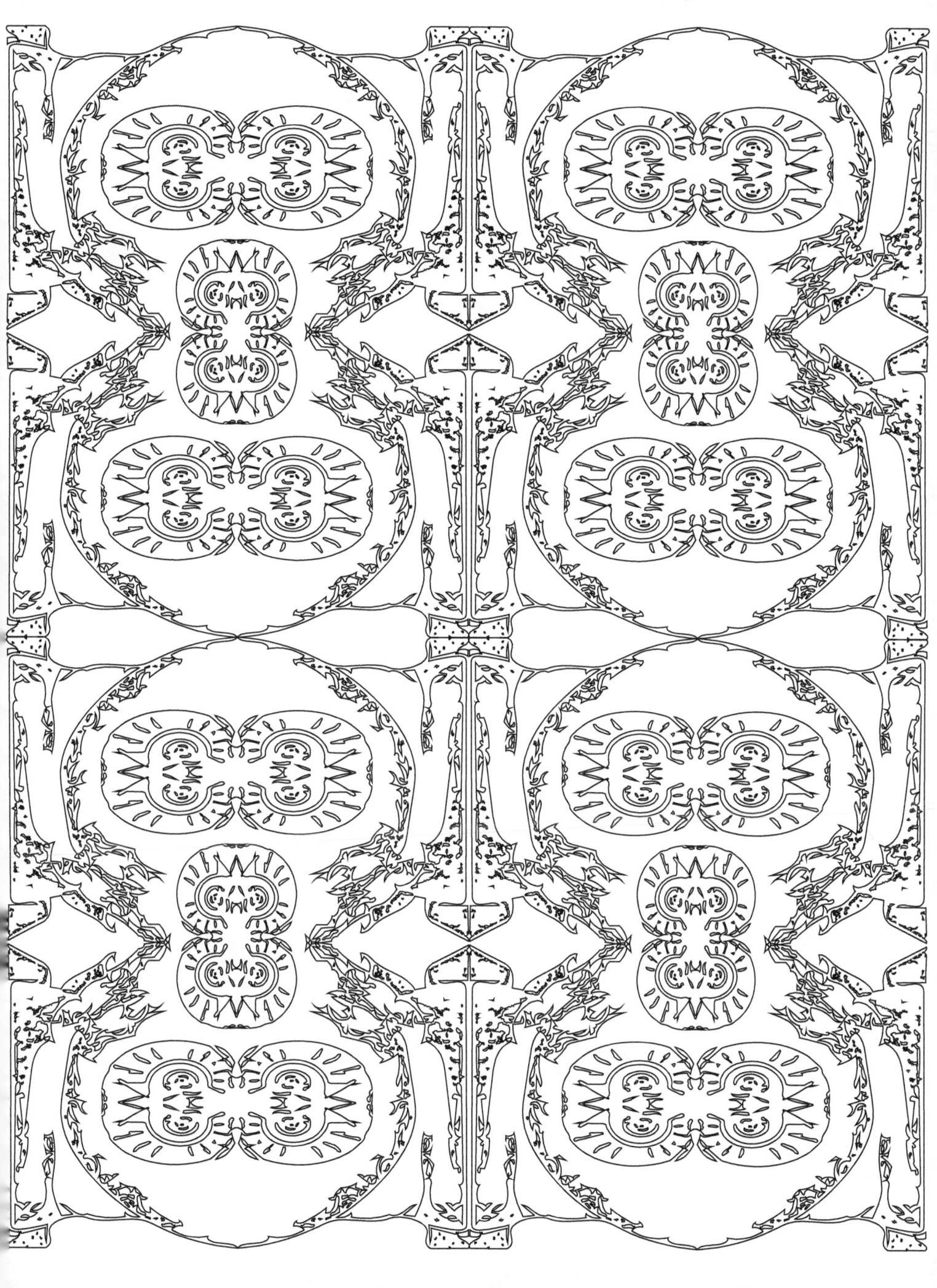

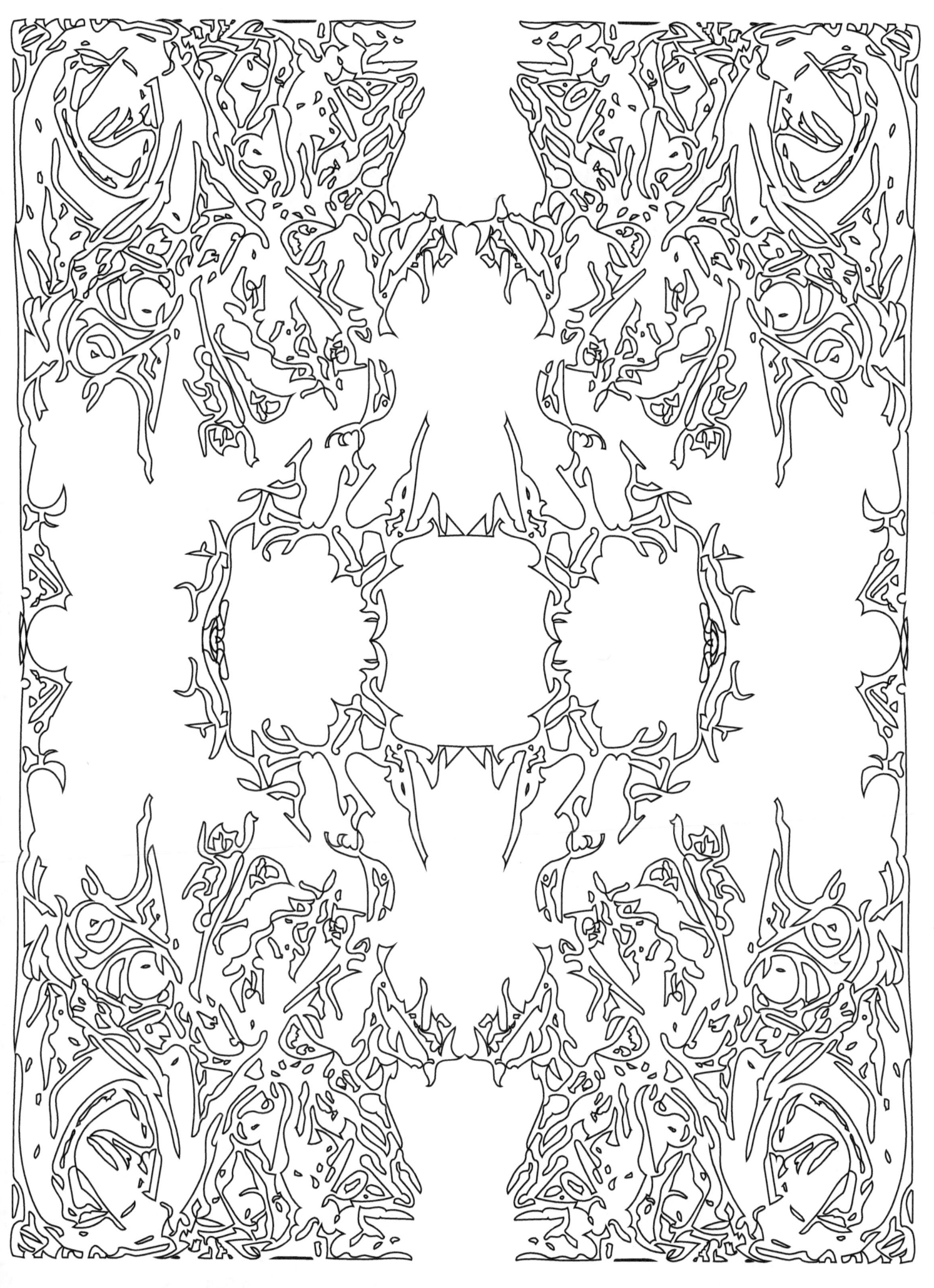

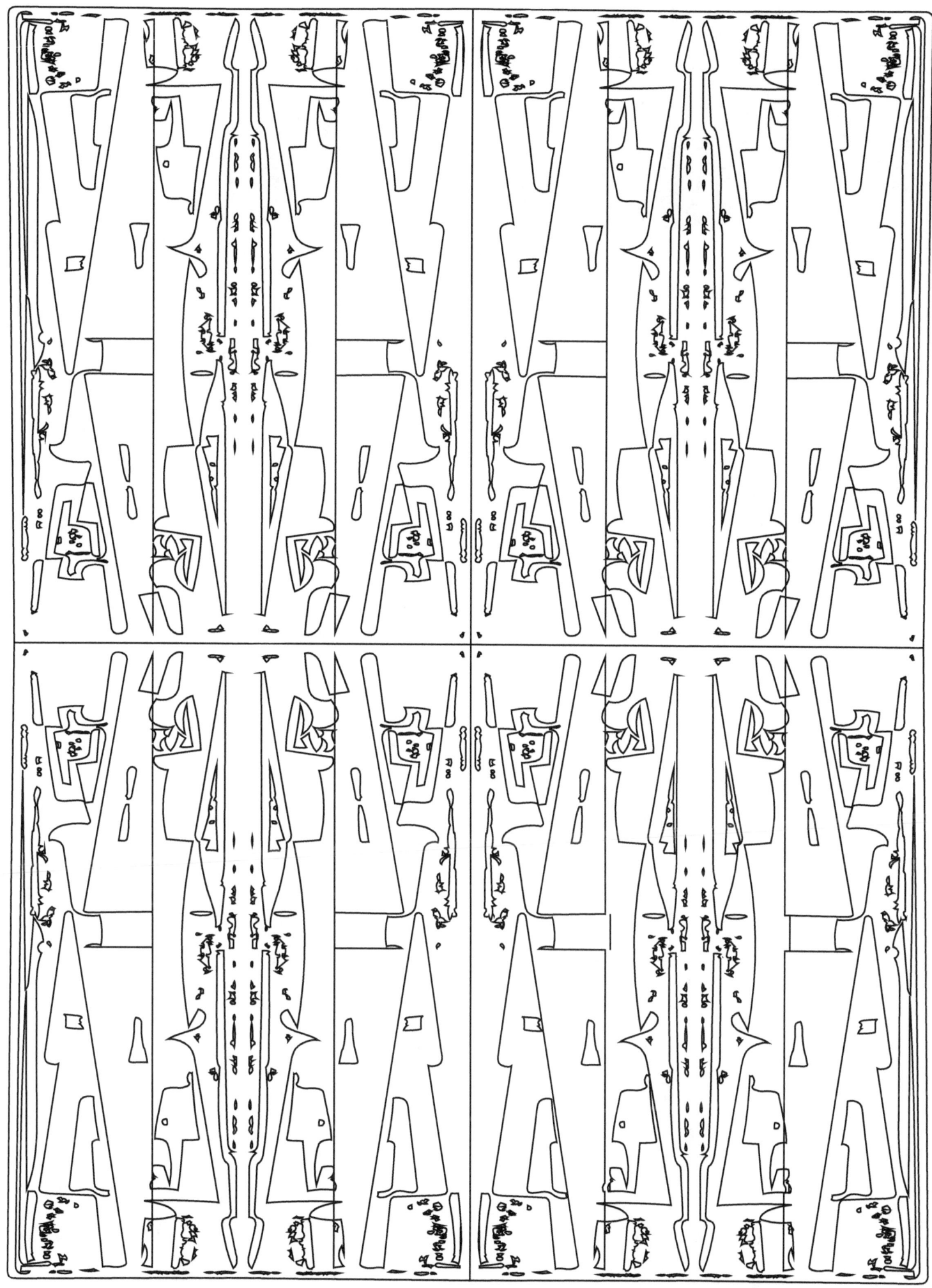

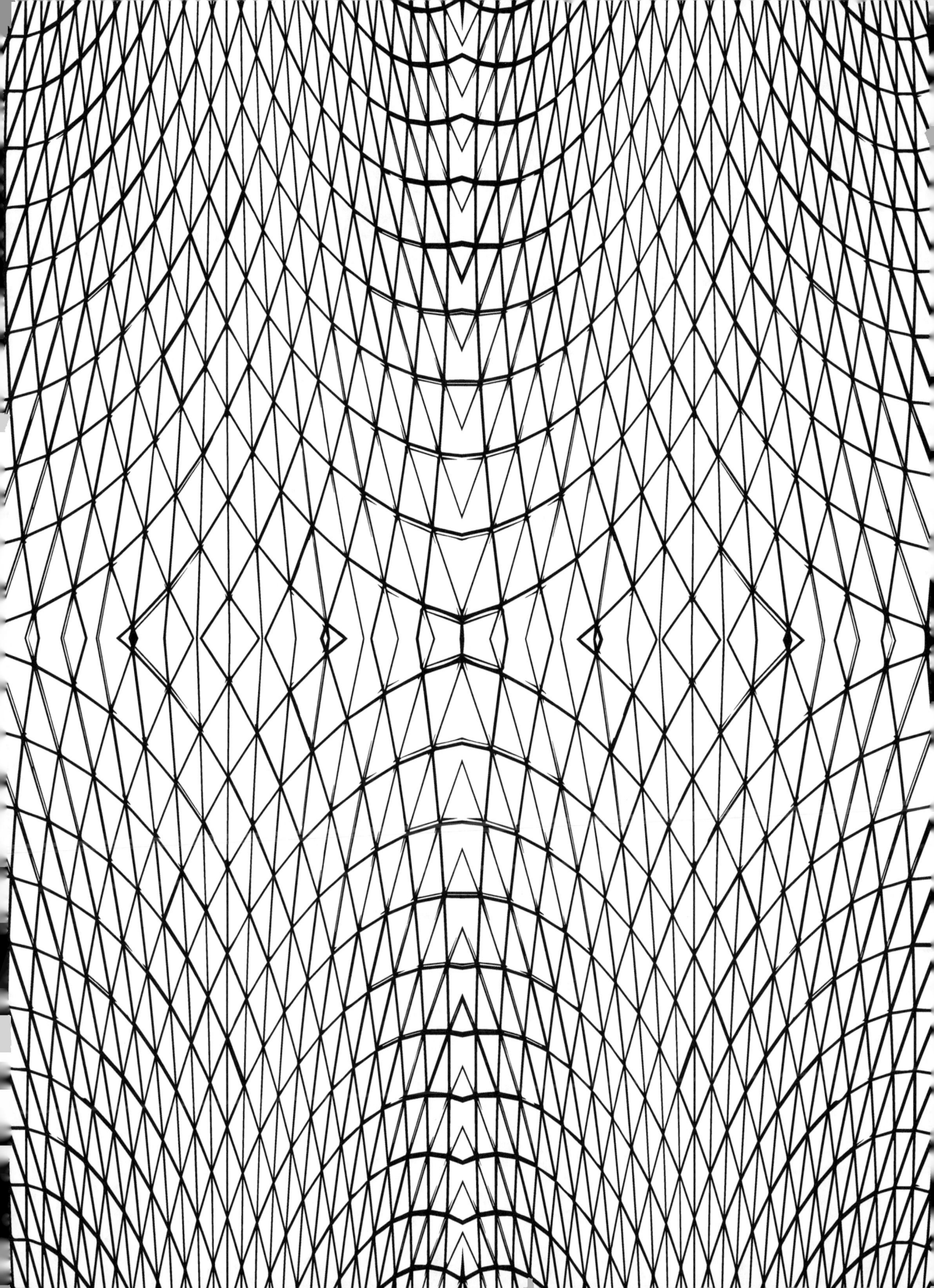

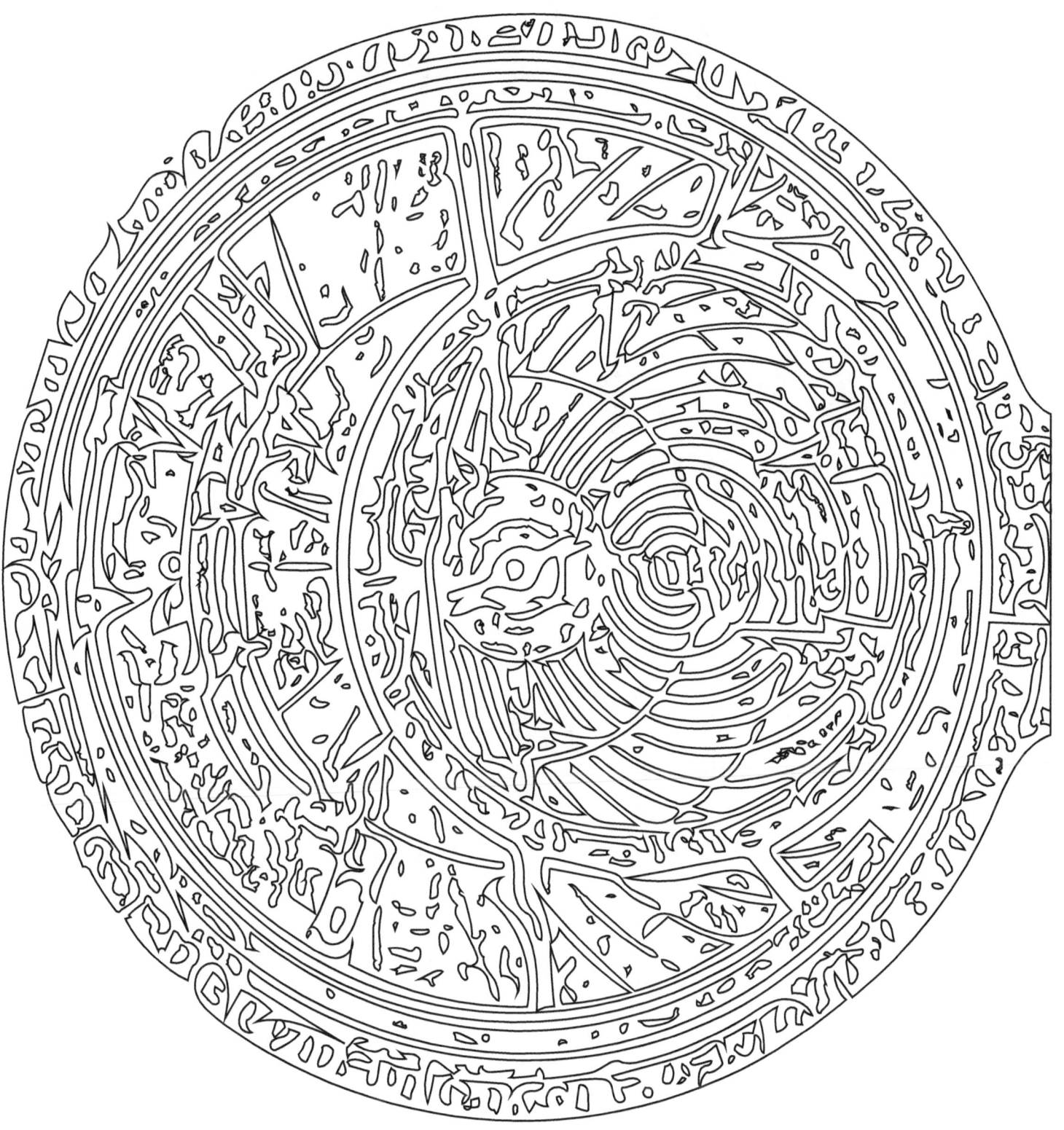

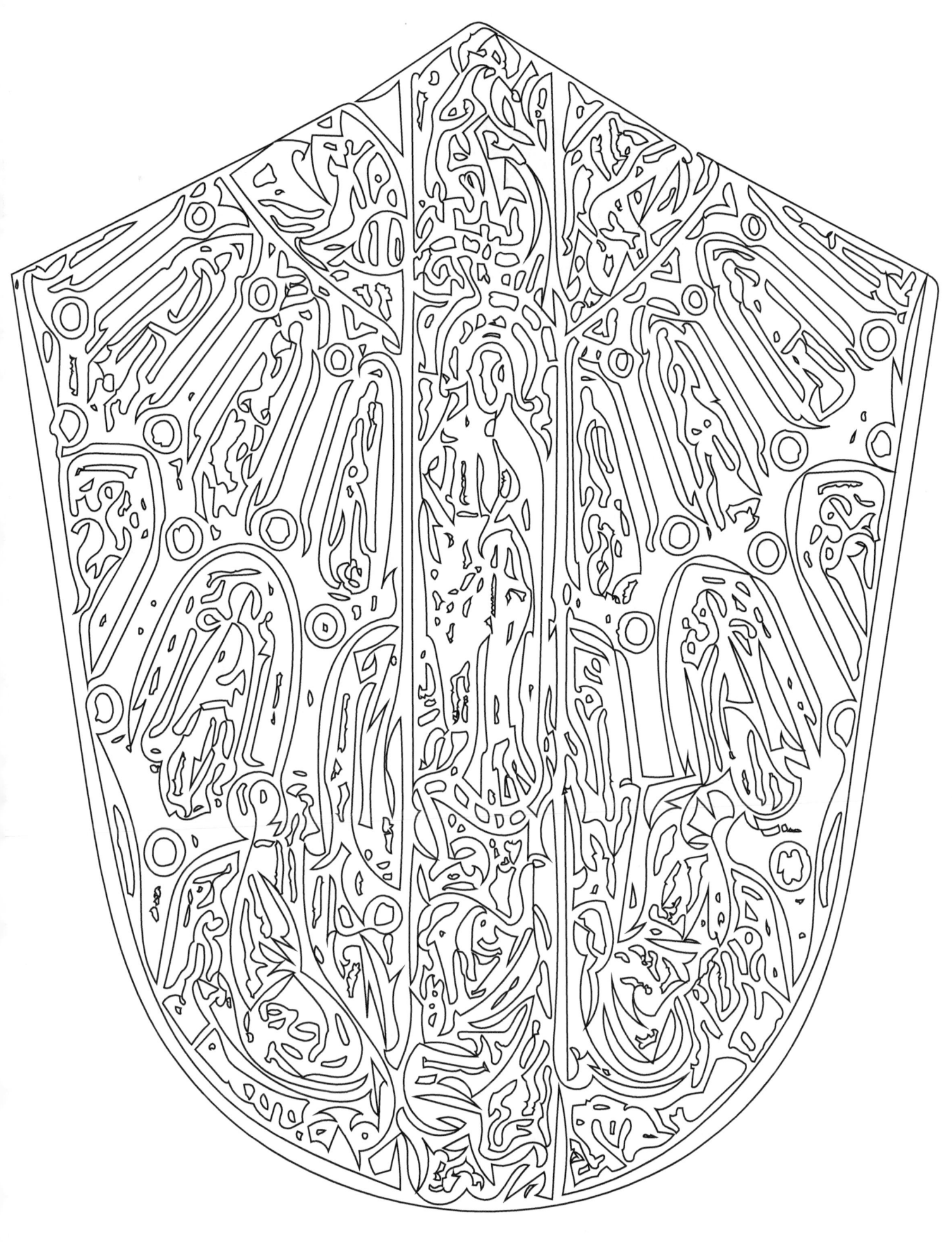

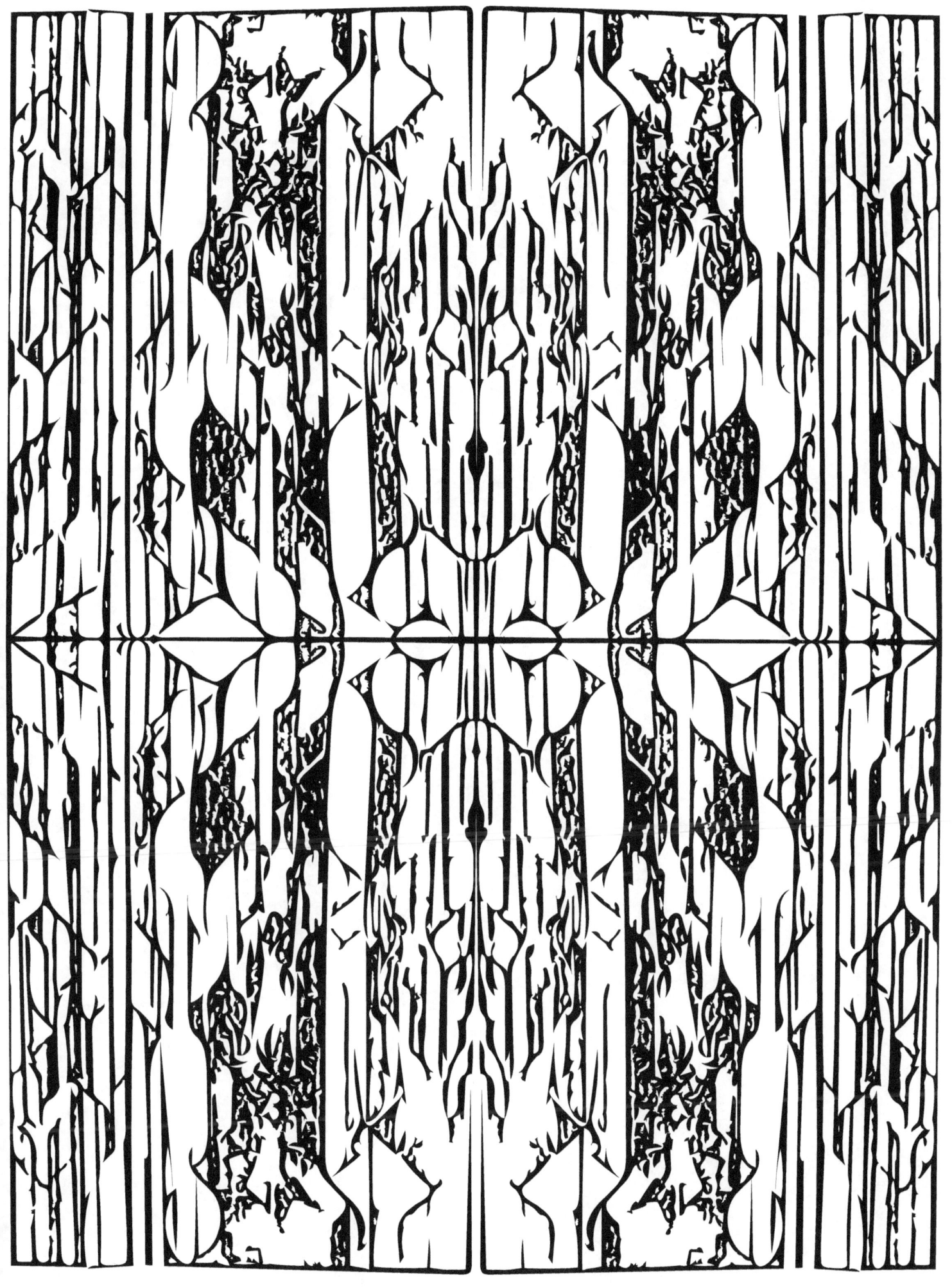

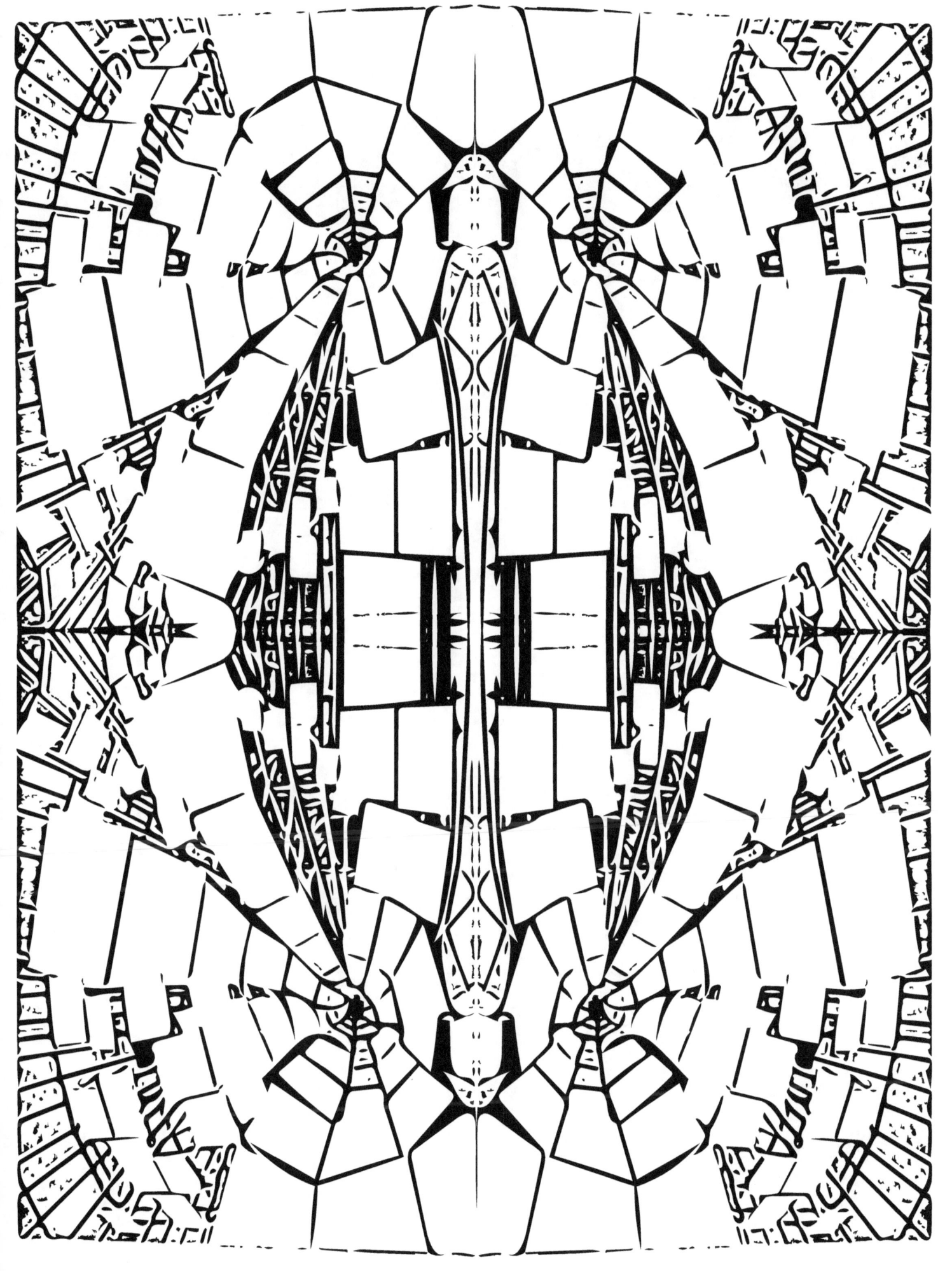

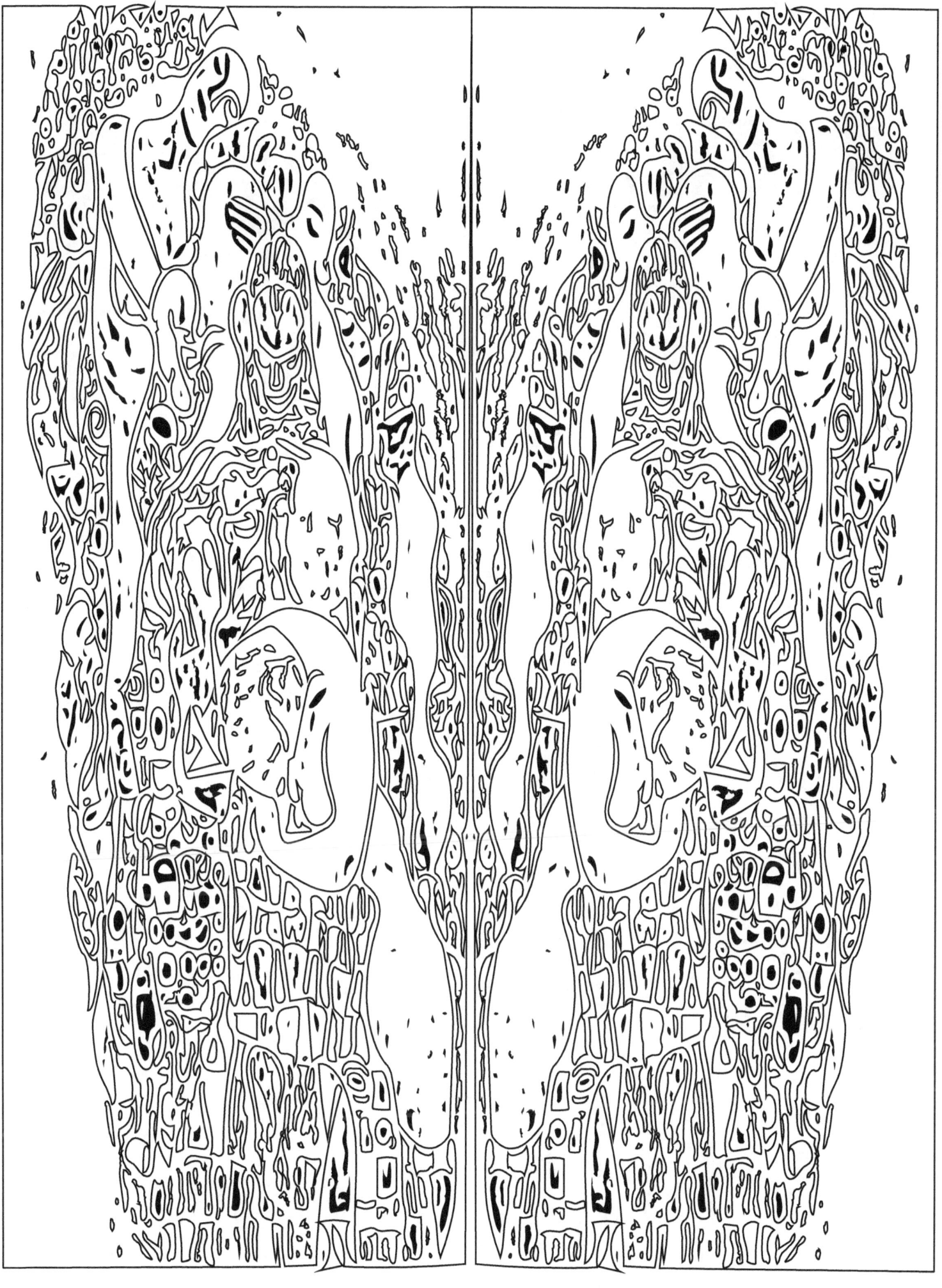

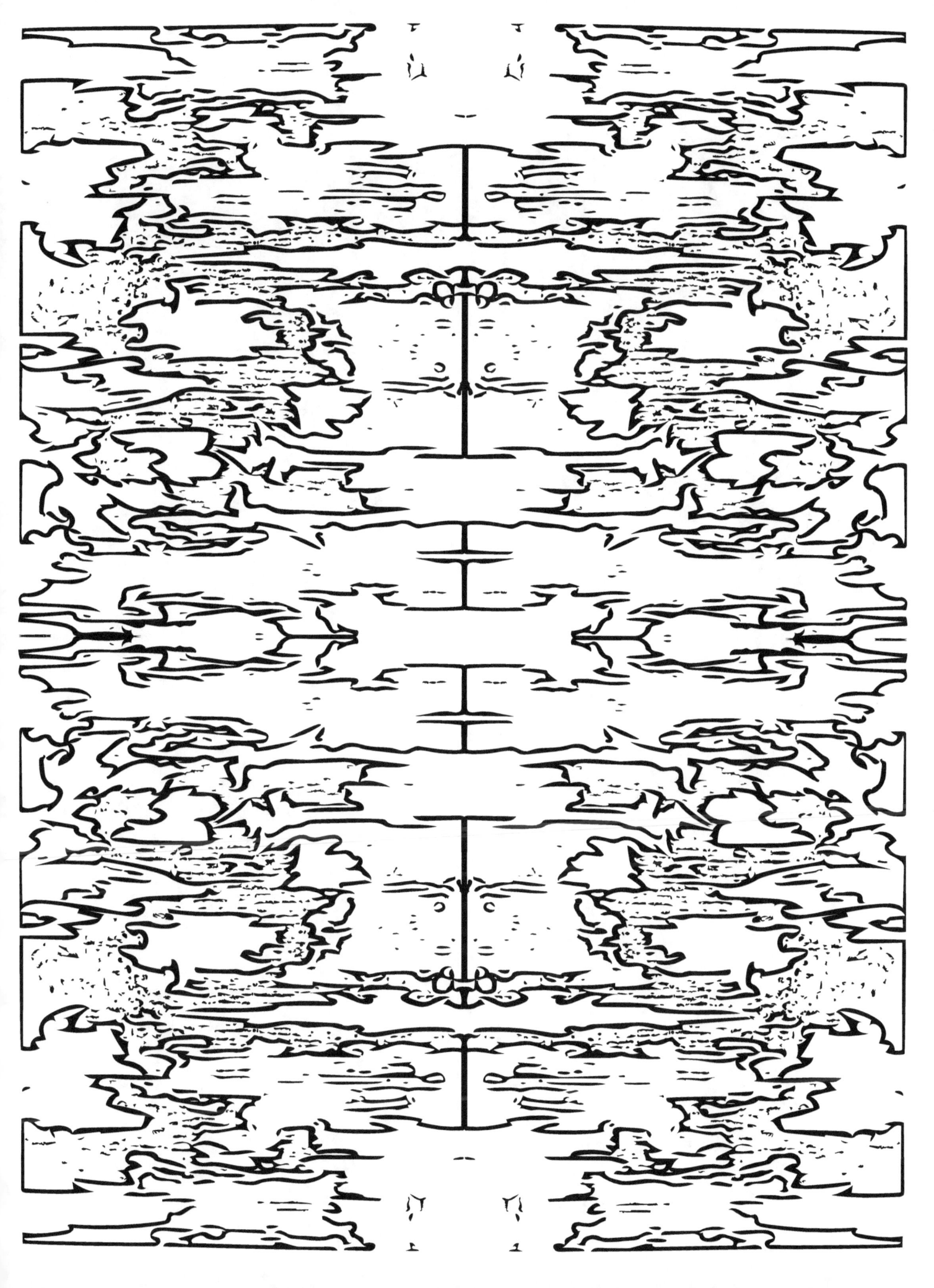

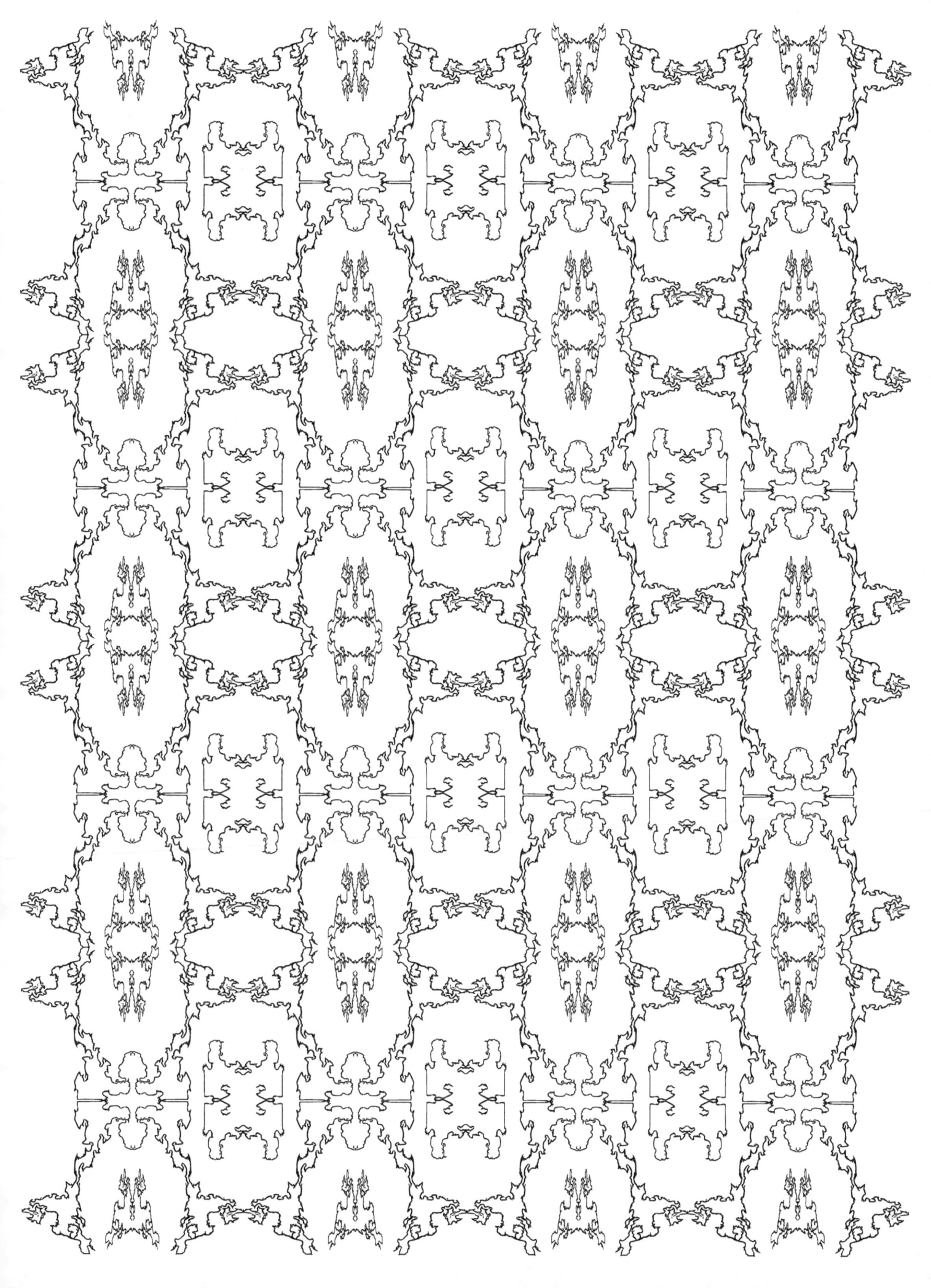

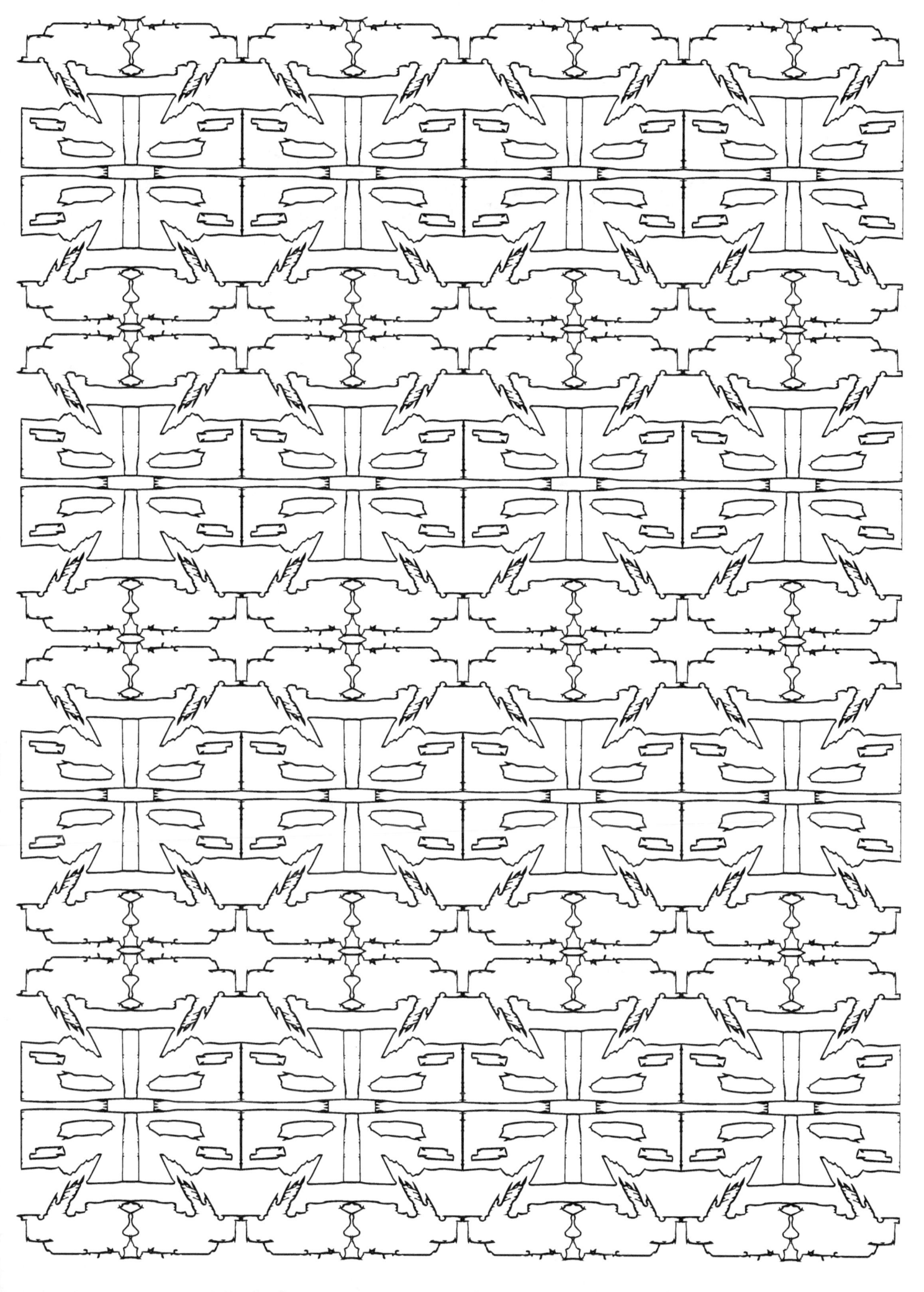

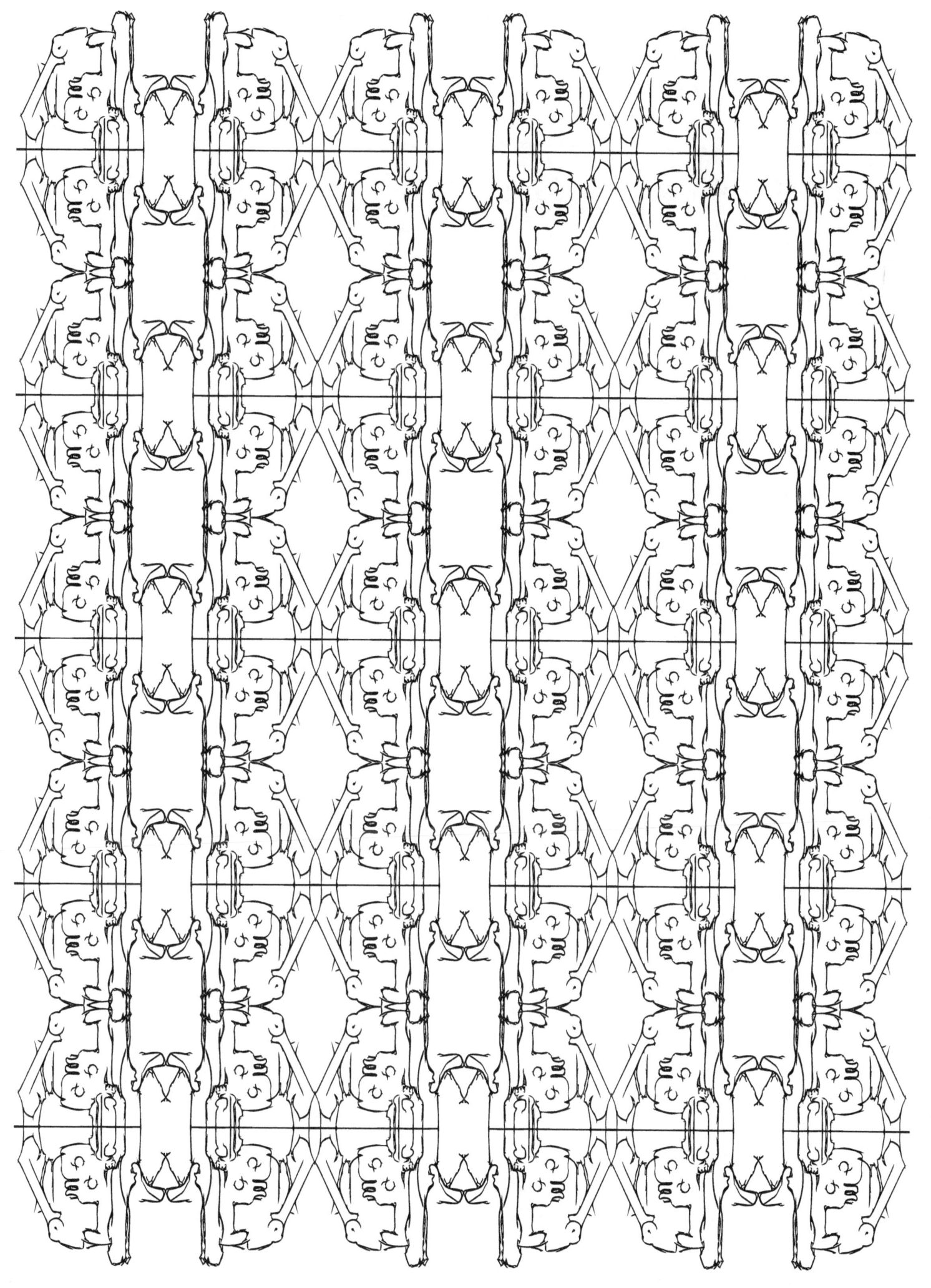

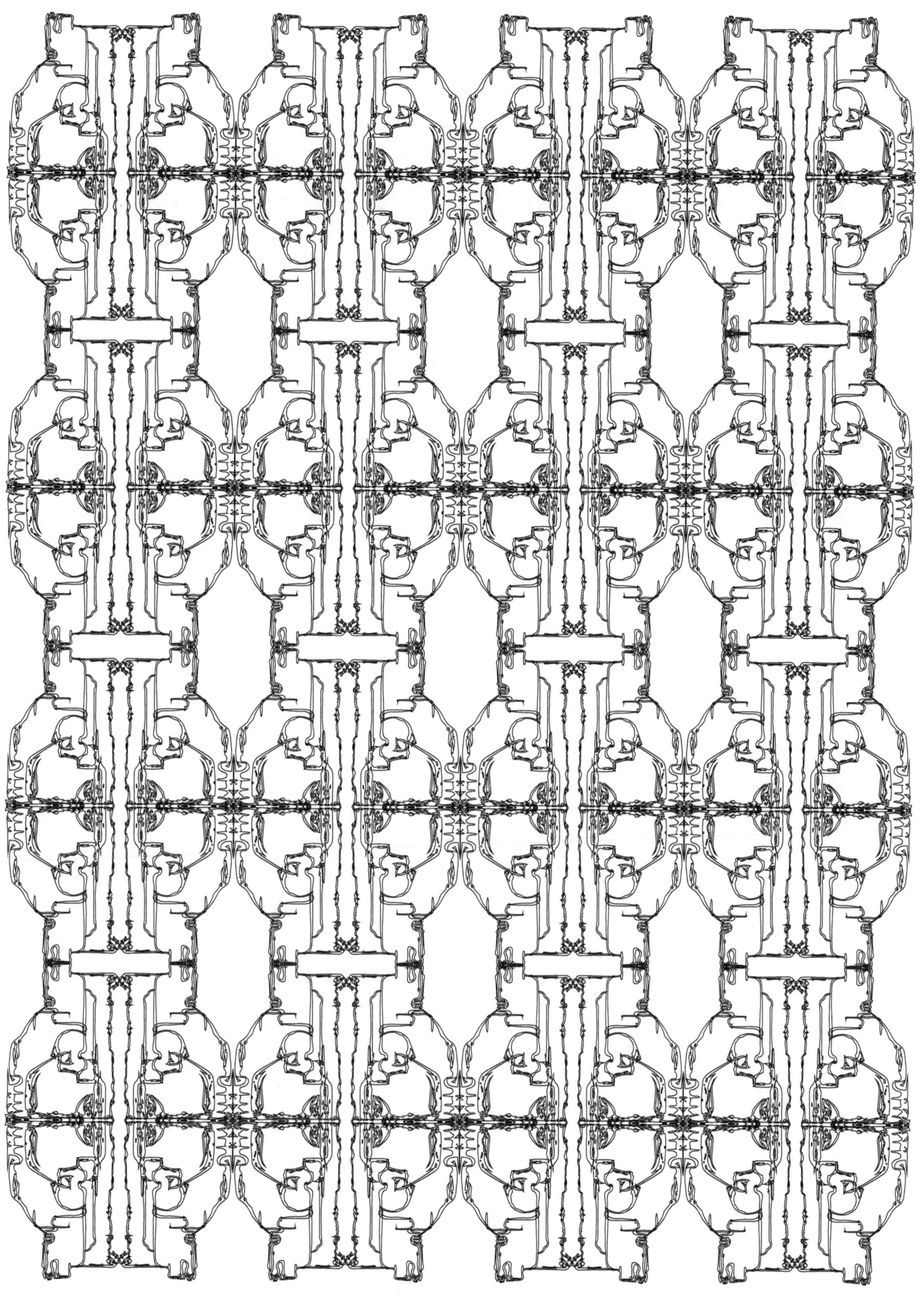

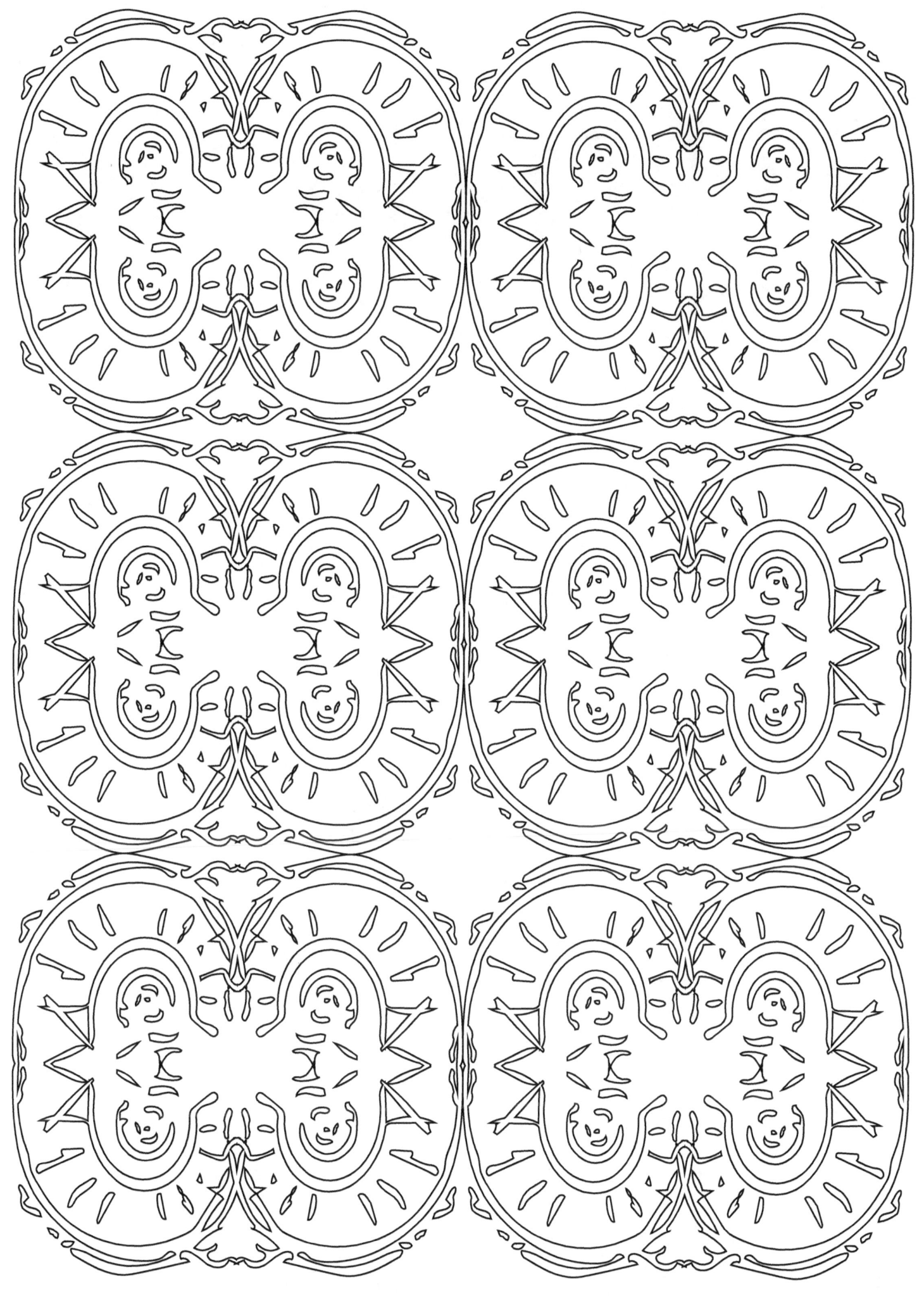

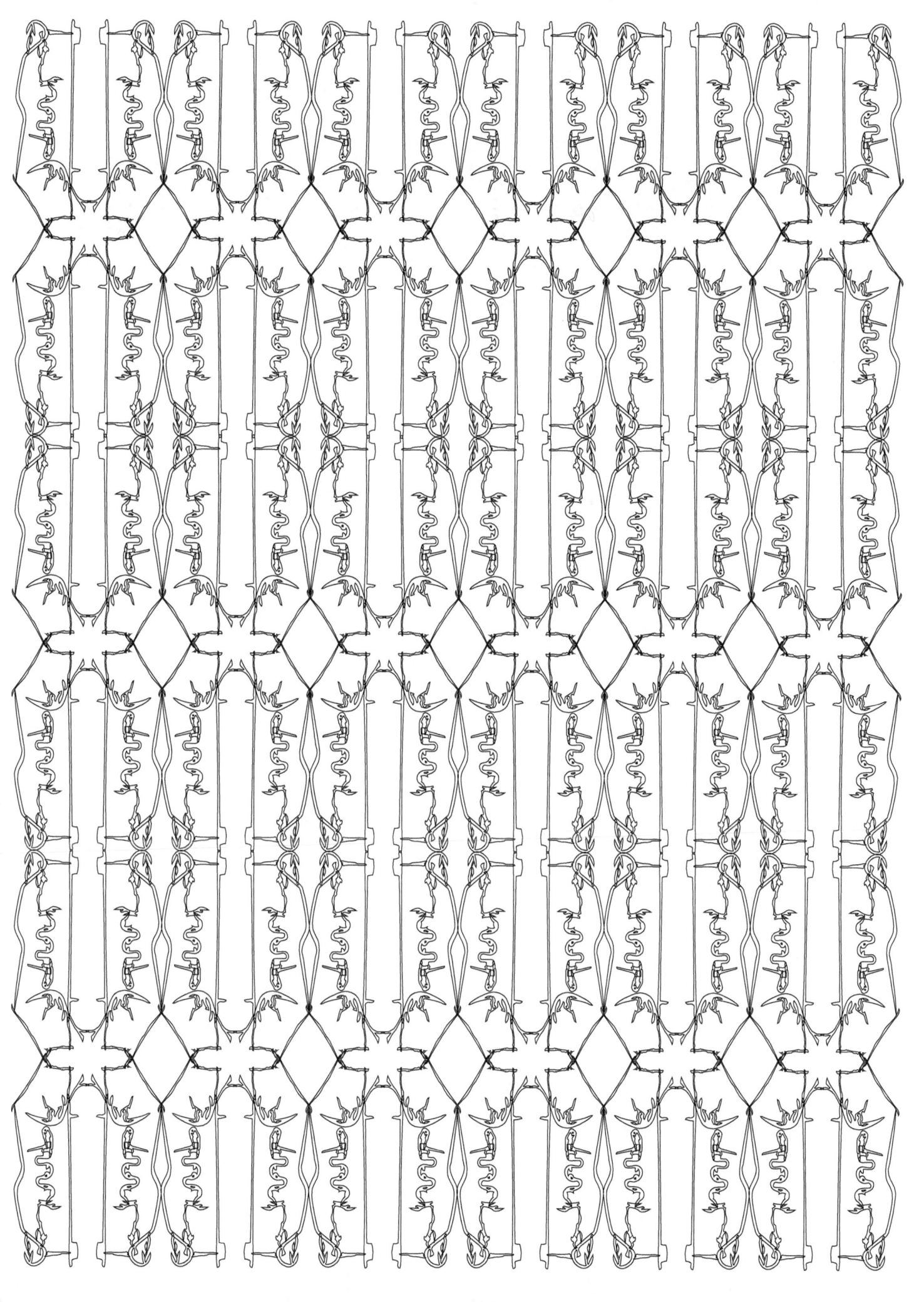

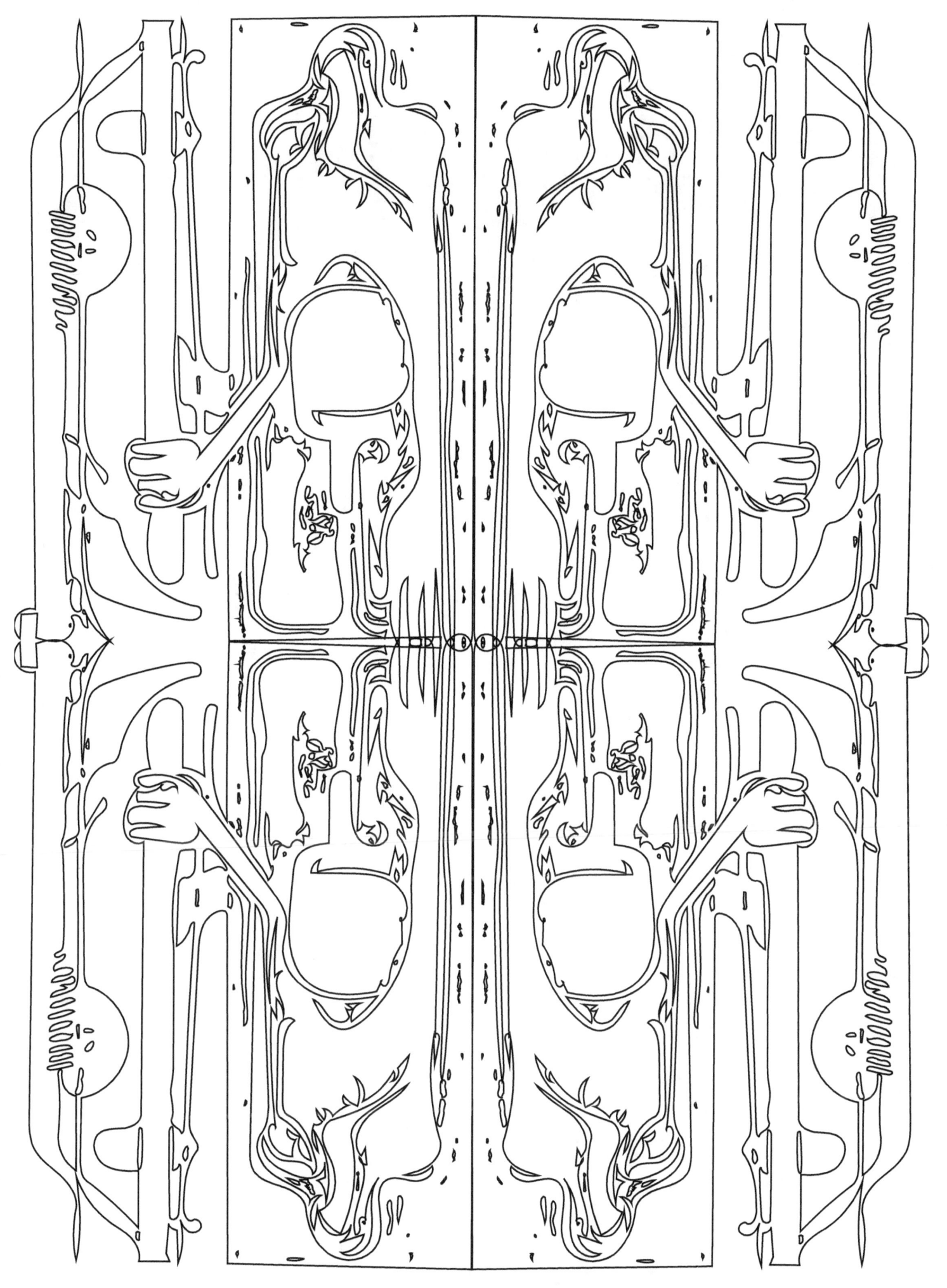

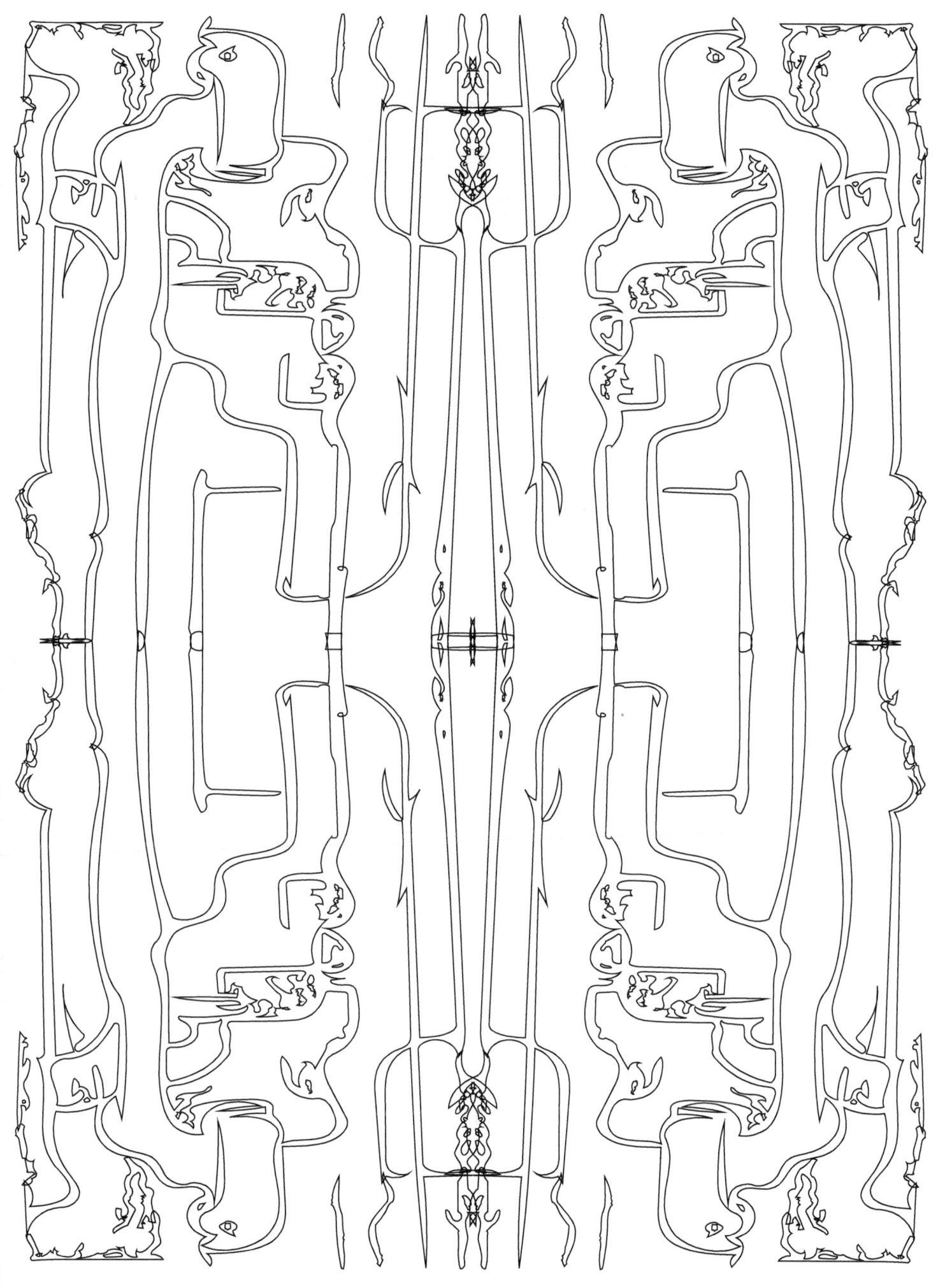

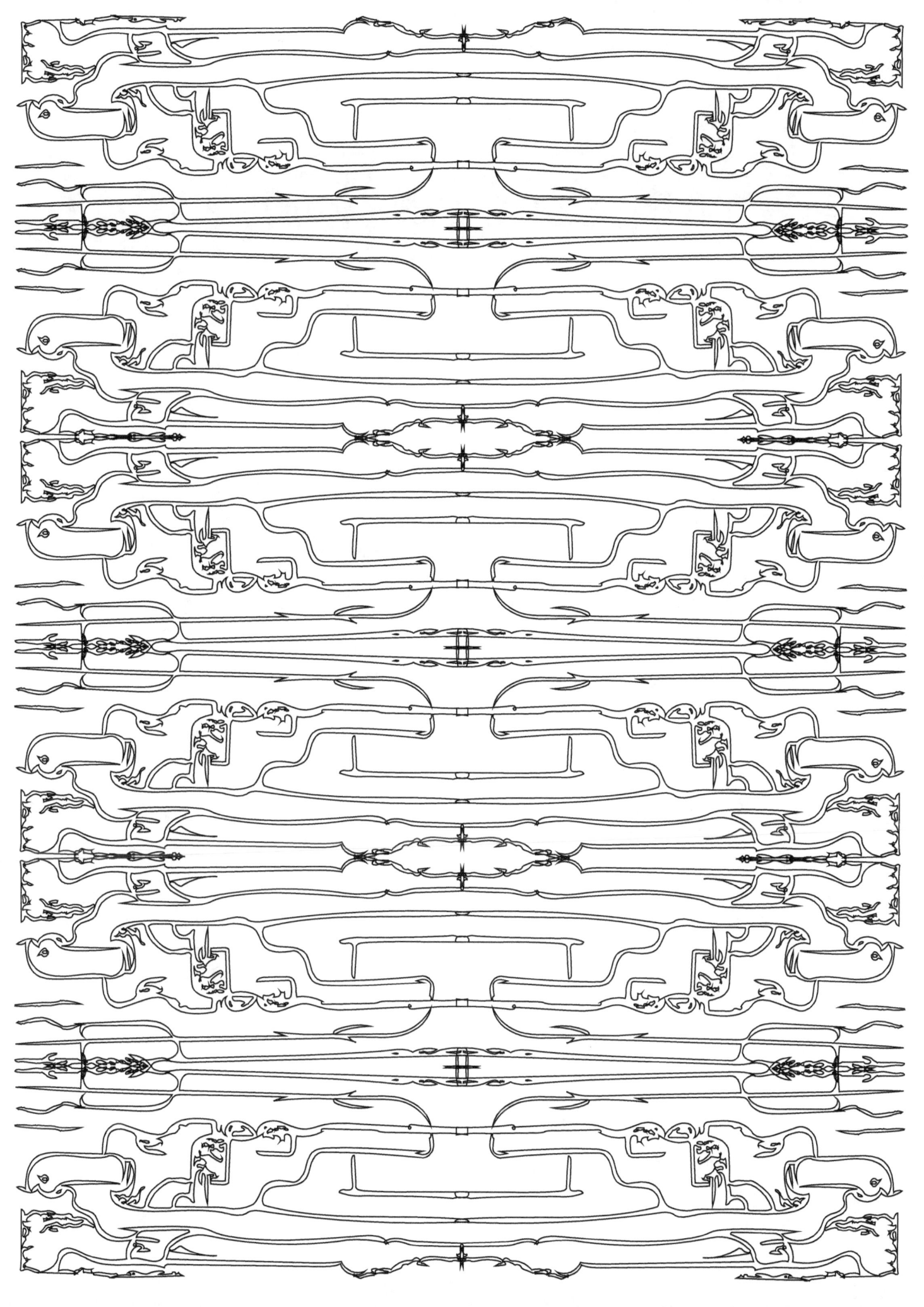

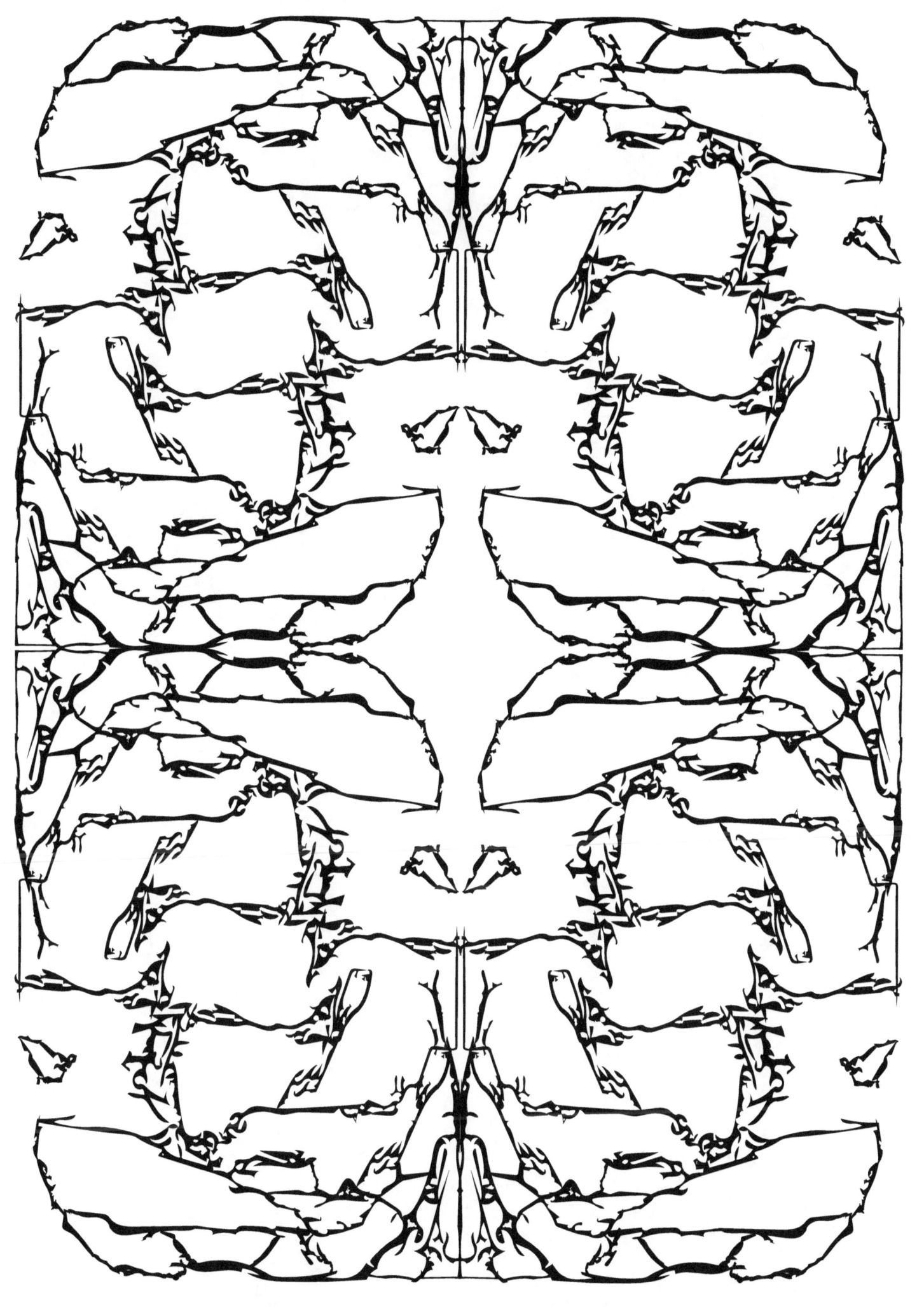

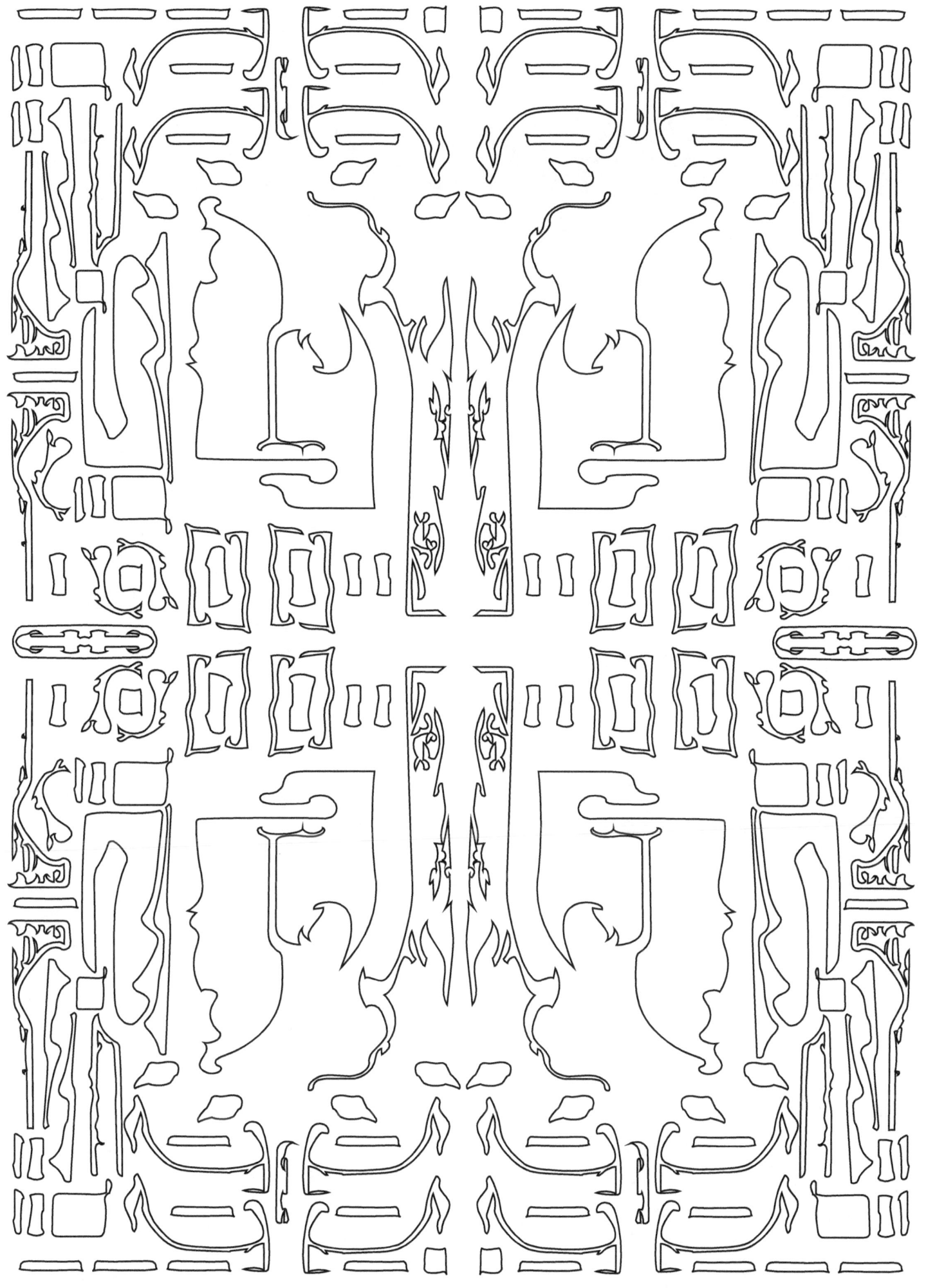

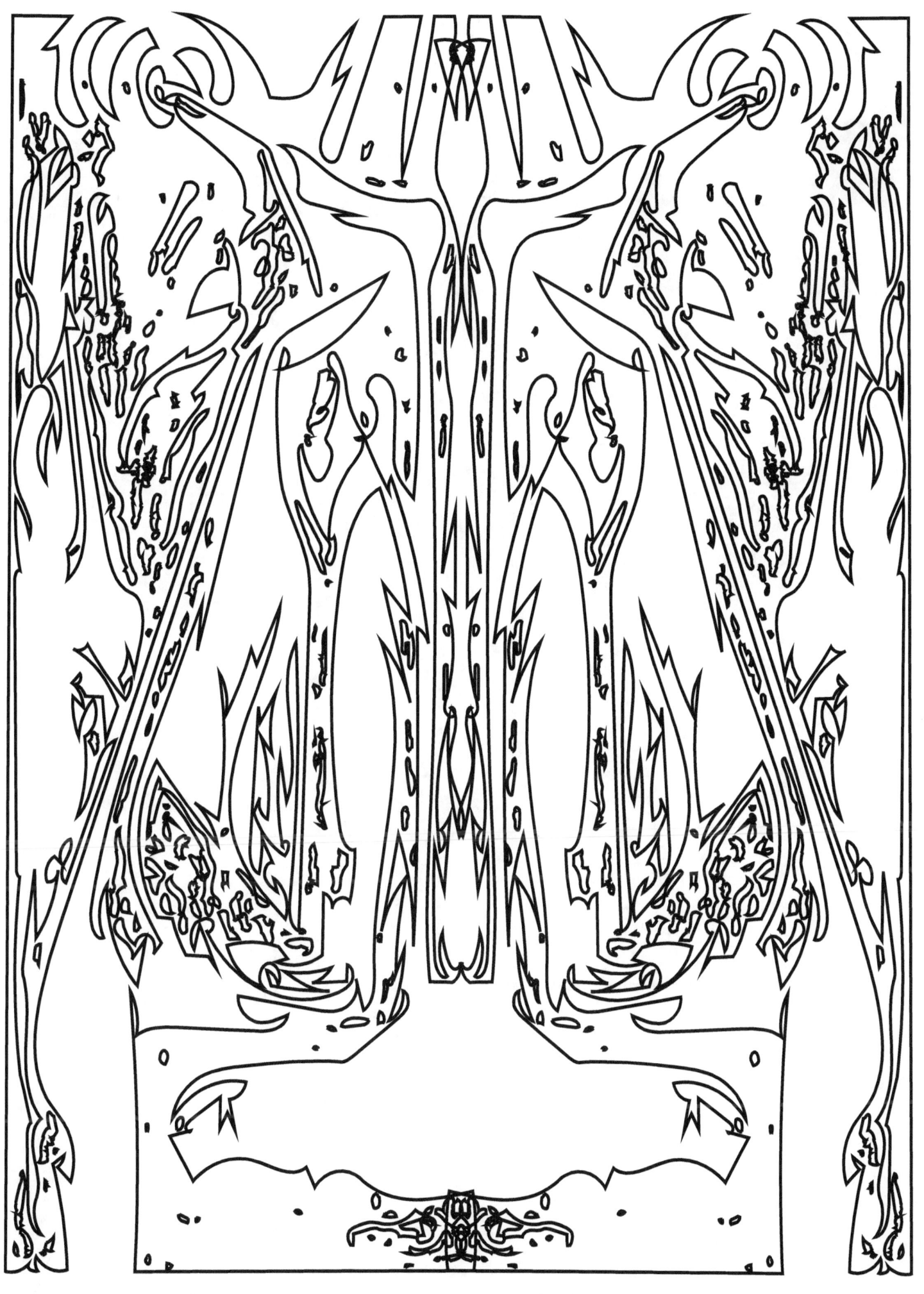

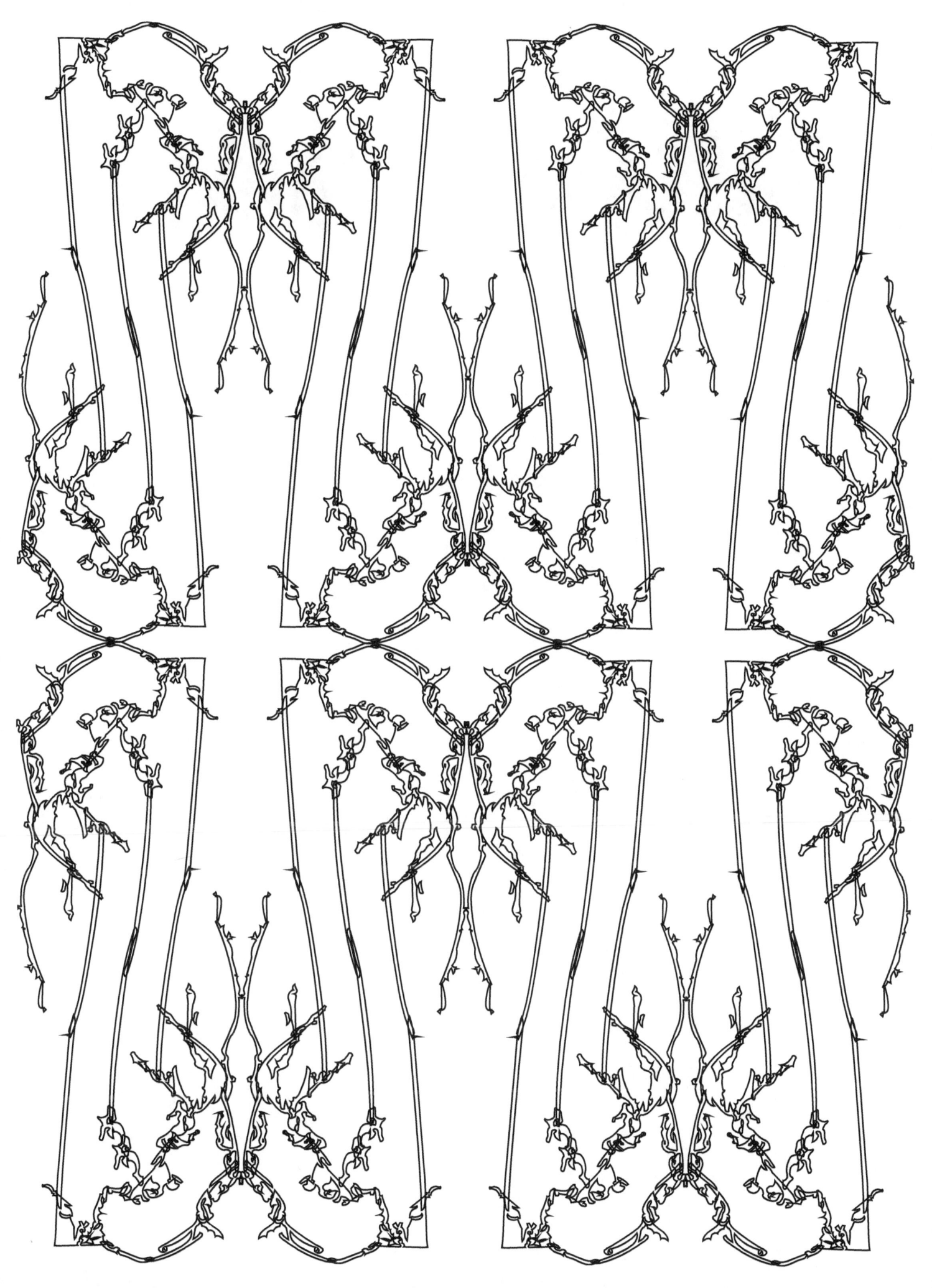

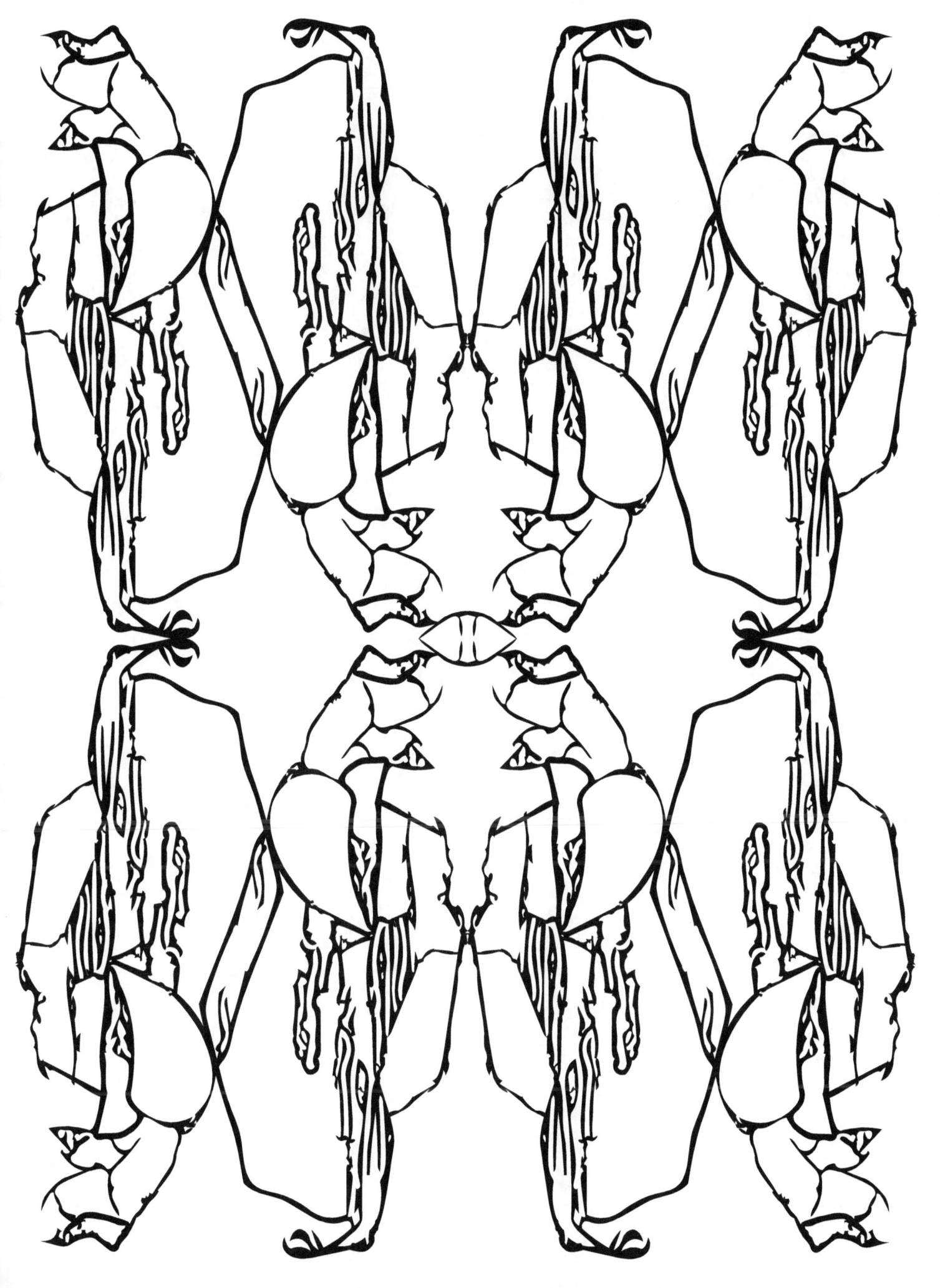

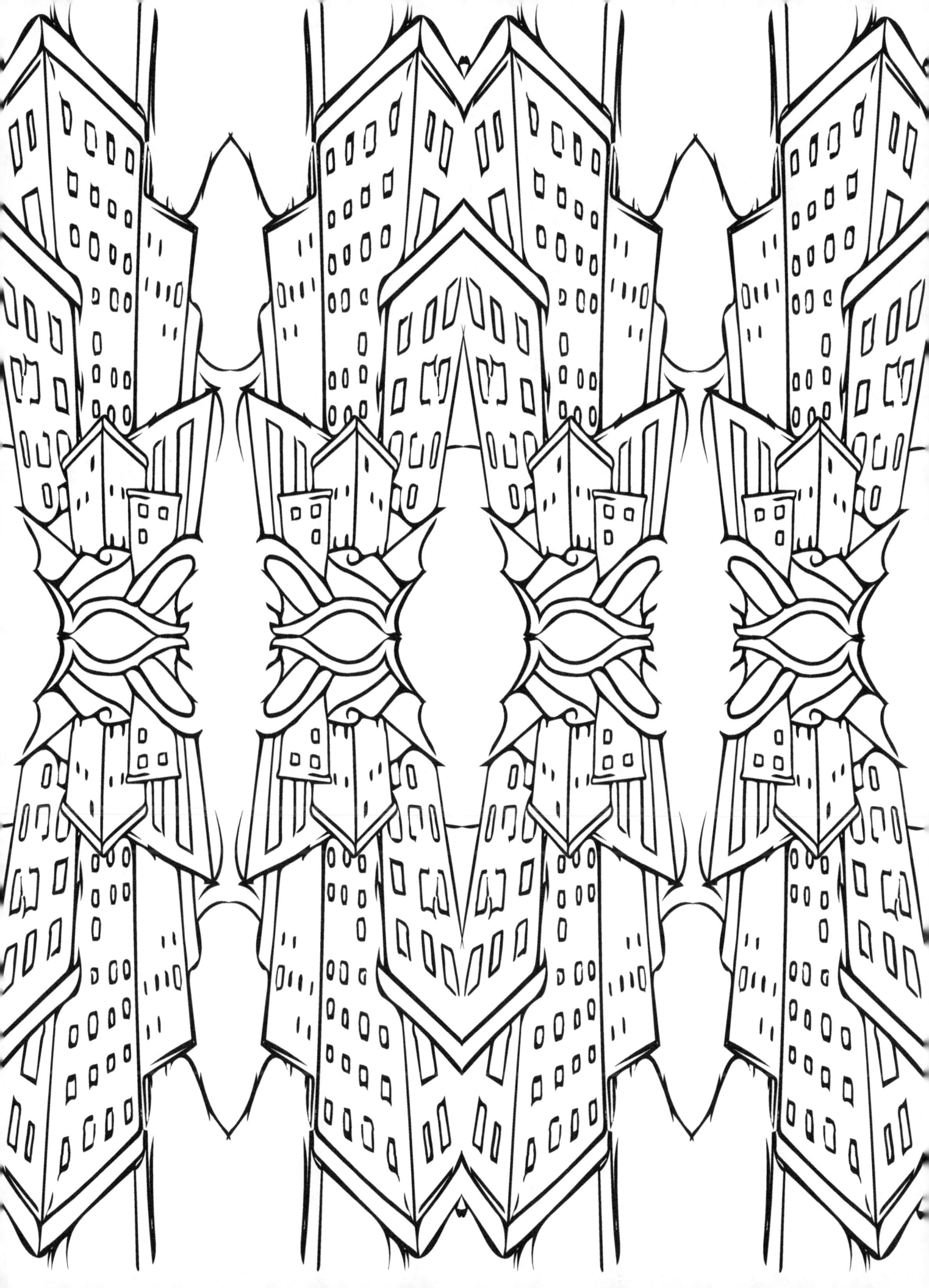

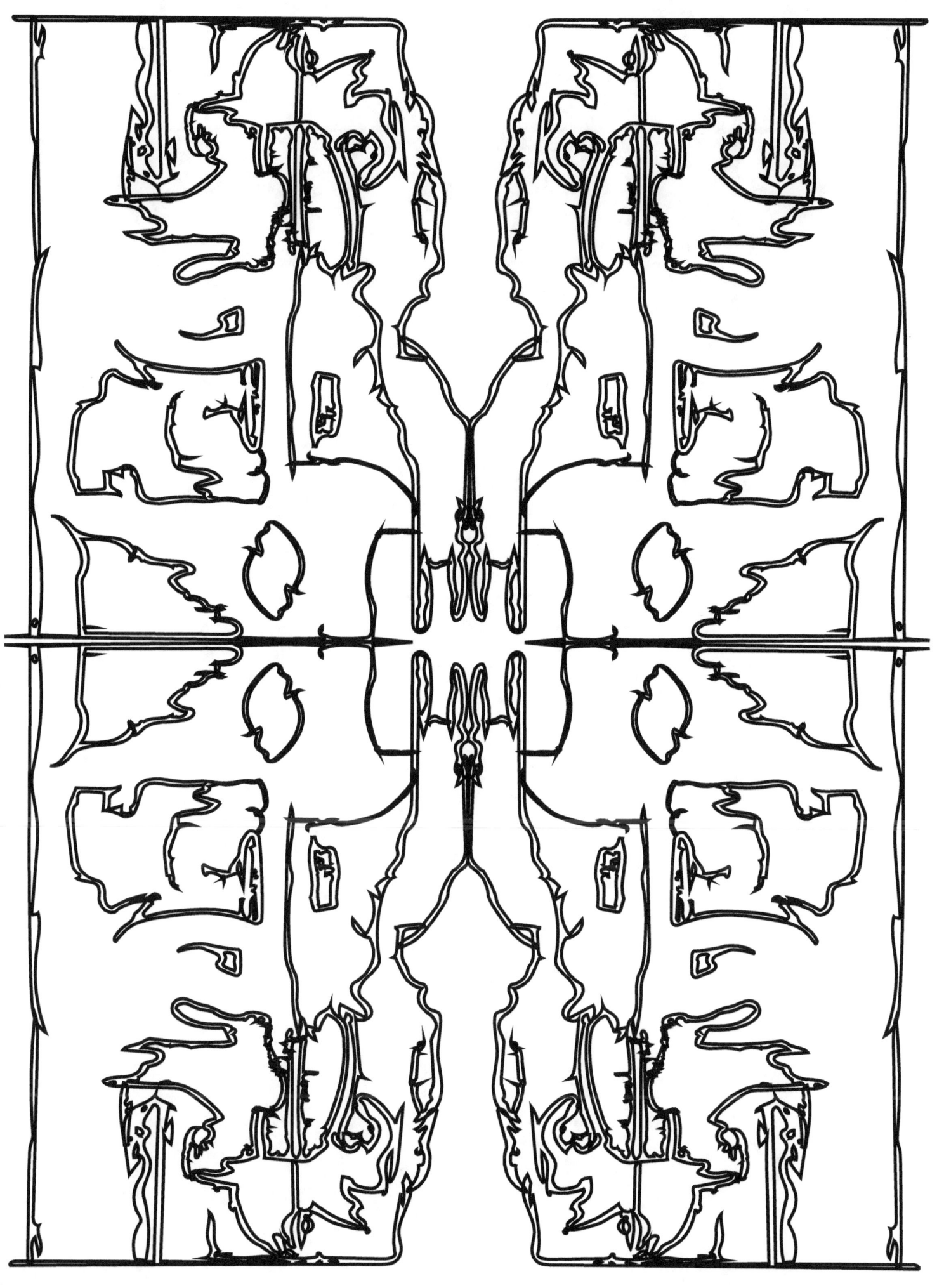

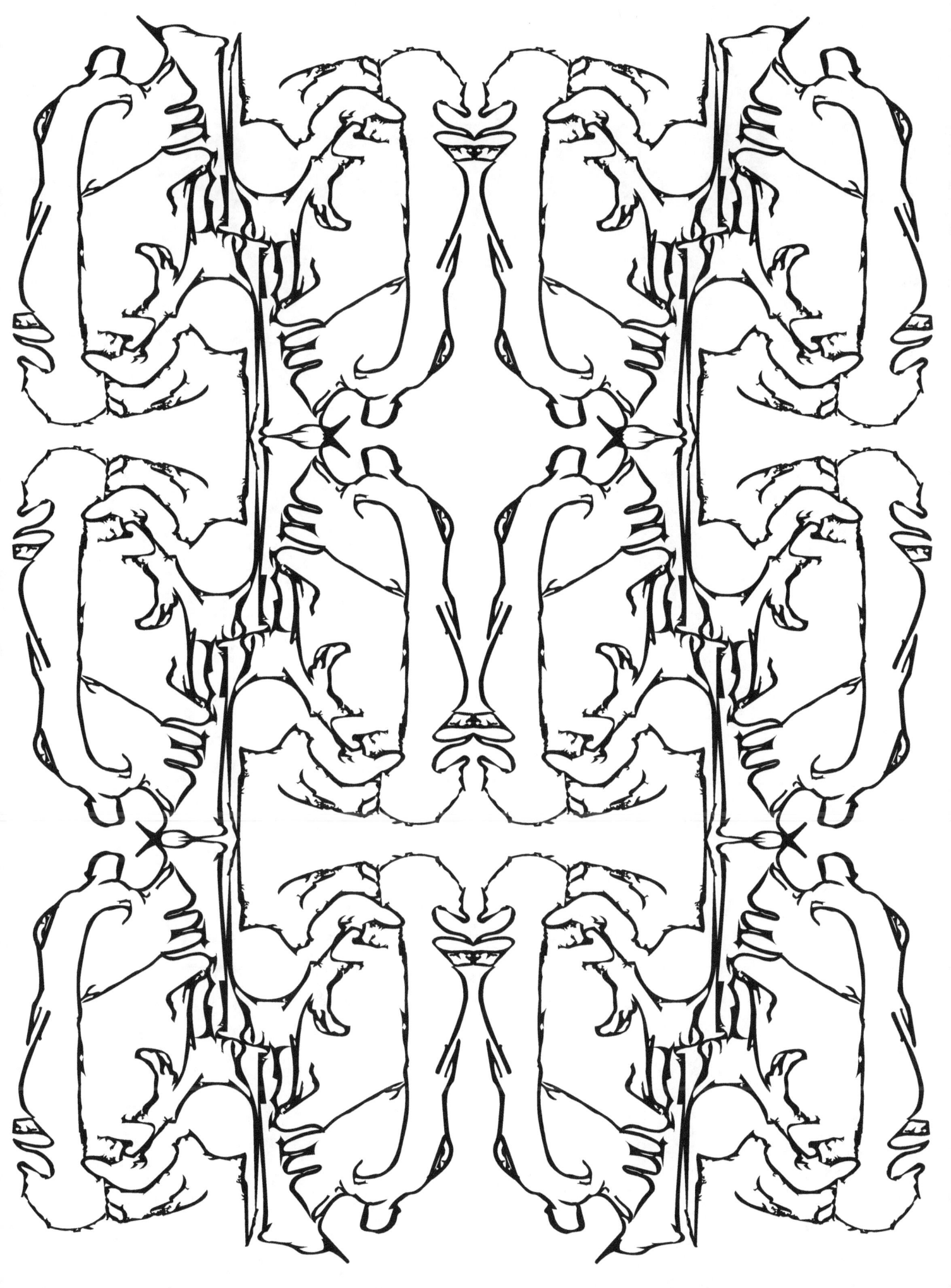

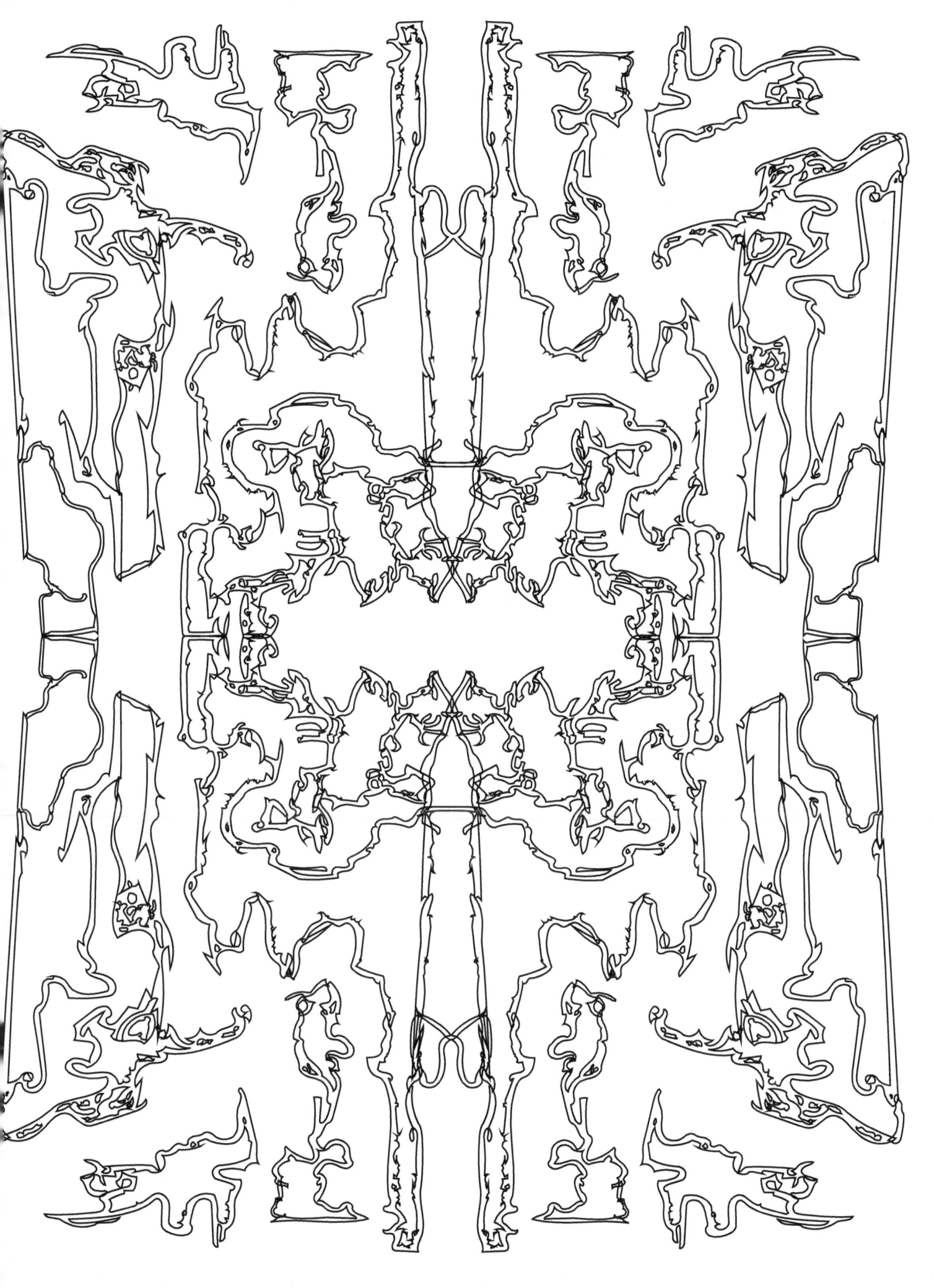

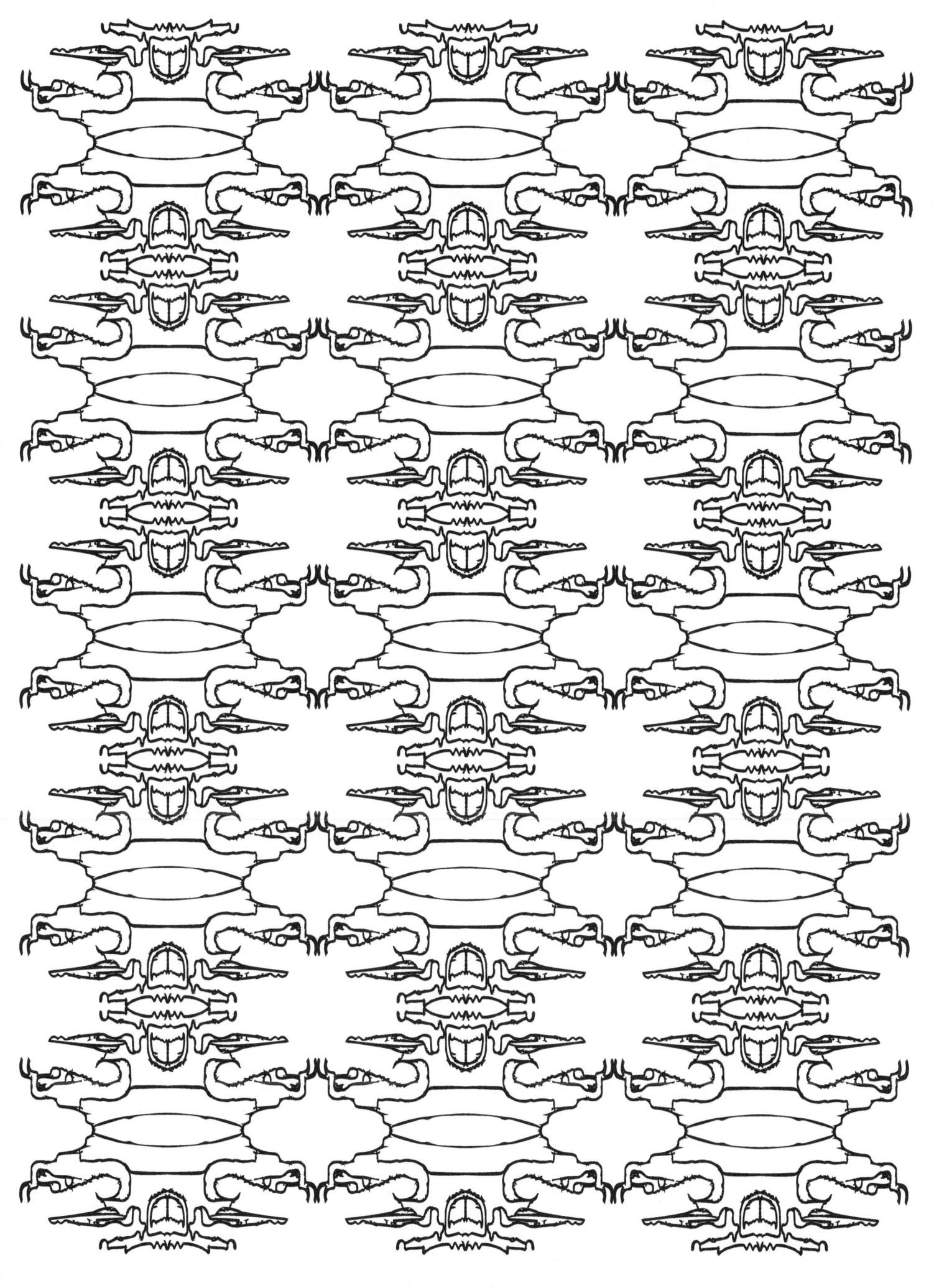

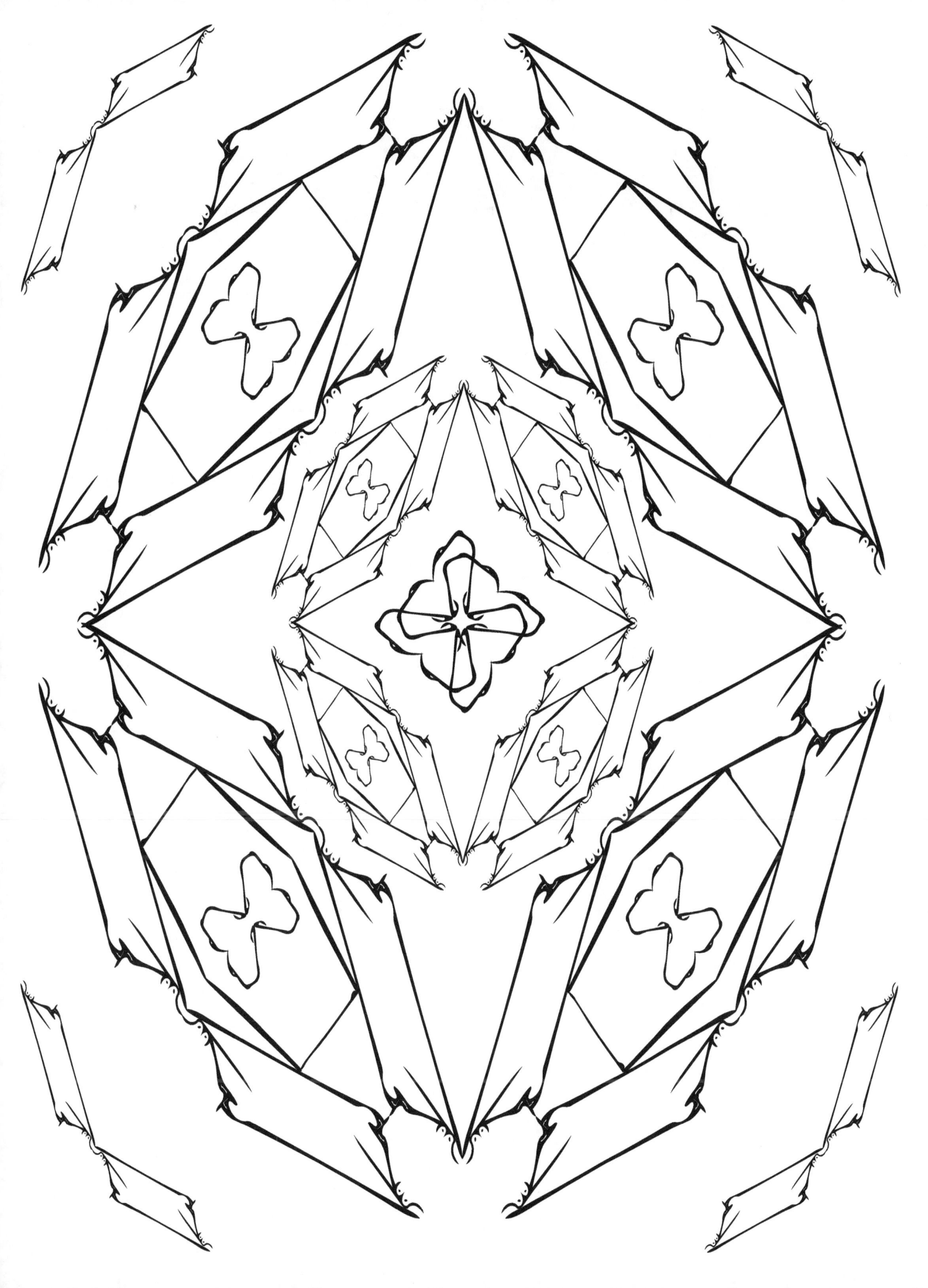

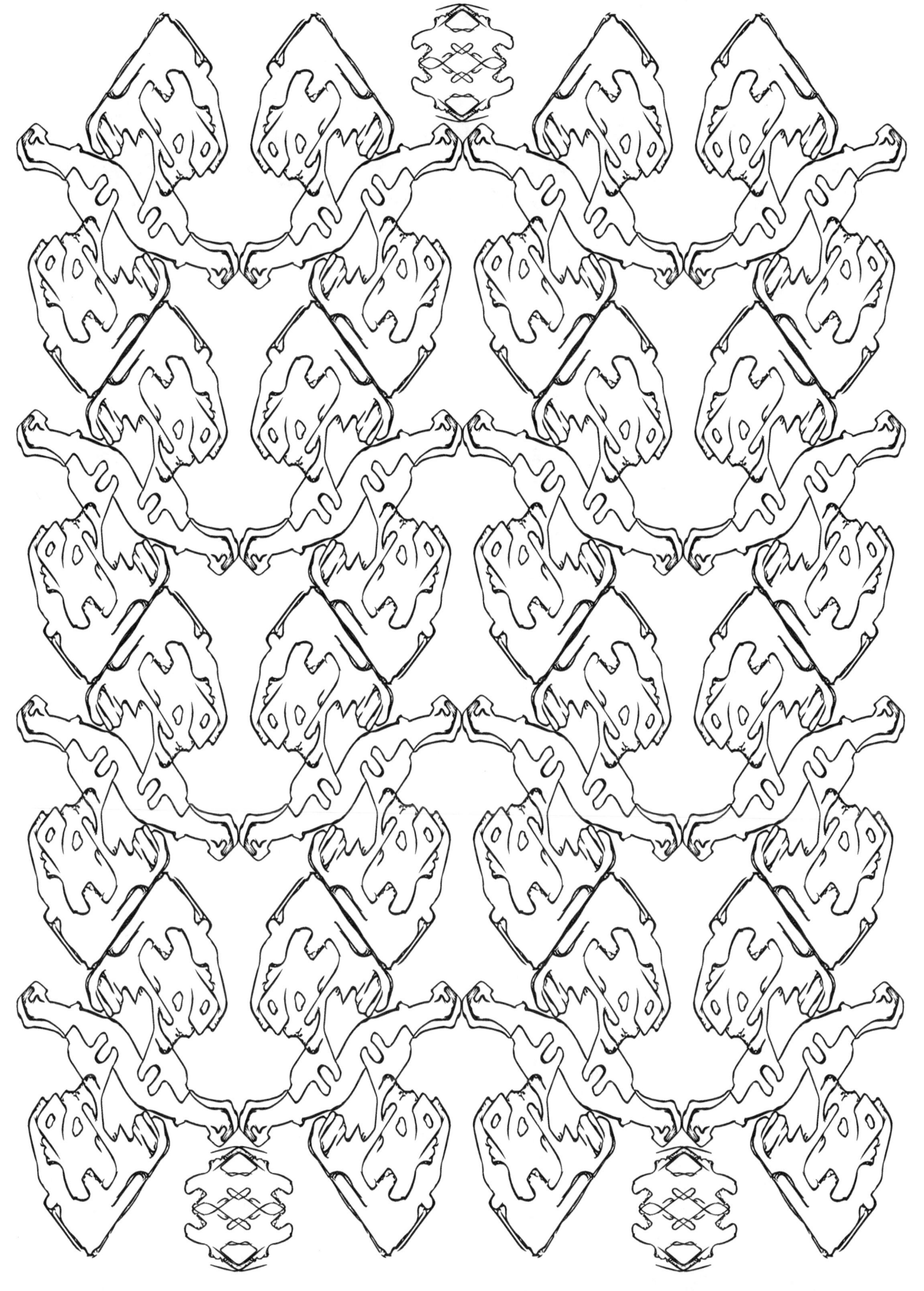

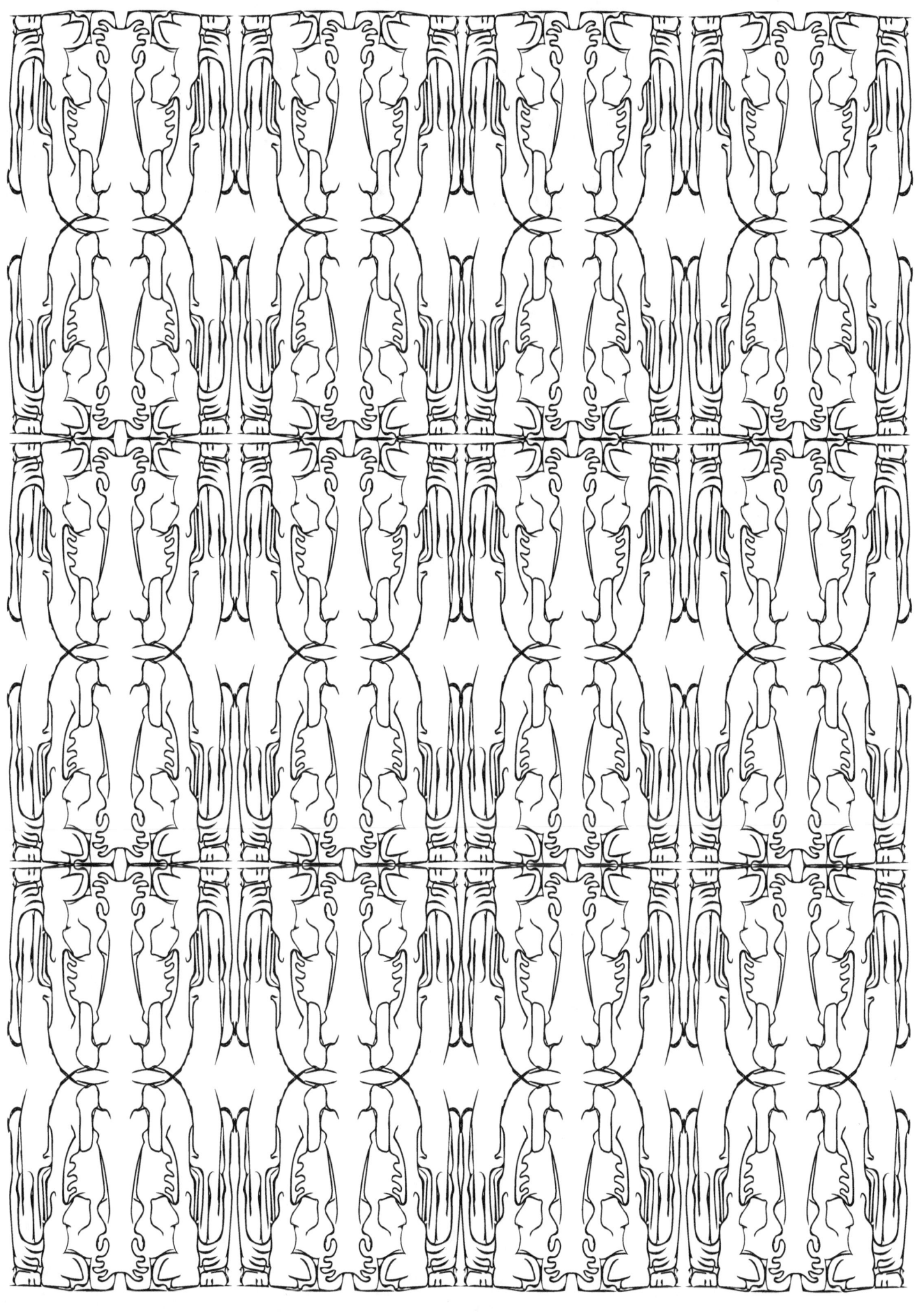

www.ingramcontent.com/pod-product-compliance
Lightning Source LLC
Chambersburg PA
CBHW080711190526
45169CB00006B/2335